THE
RESOLUTION
for MEN
BIBLE STUDY

By Stephen Kendrick and Alex Kendrick
As developed with Travis Agnew

B&H Publishing Group
Nashville, Tennessee

Published by LifeWay Press® Copyright © 2013 Stephen Kendrick and Alex Kendrick

ISBN: 978-1-4158-7227-7
Item: 005471374
Dewey Decimal Classification: 248.842
Subject Headings: MEN \ DISCIPLESHIP \ CHRISTIAN LIFE

To order additional copies of this resource, write to LifeWay Church Resources Customer Service, One LifeWay Plaza, Nashville TN 37234-0113; fax 615.251.5933; phone toll free 800.458.2772; order online at *www.lifeway.com*; email *orderentry@lifeway.com*; or visit the LifeWay Christian Store serving you.

Printed in the United States of America.

Adult Ministry Publishing
LifeWay Church Resources
One LifeWay Plaza
Nashville, TN 37234-0152

CONTENTS

ABOUT THE AUTHORS

STEPHEN KENDRICK serves as senior associate pastor of preaching and prayer at Sherwood Baptist Church, Albany, Georgia (*sherwoodbaptist. net*). He is cowriter and producer of Sherwood Pictures' movies, including *FIREPROOF* and *COURAGEOUS*.

Stephen and his brother, Alex, cowrote *Honor Begins at Home, Courageous Living Bible Study*, and *The Resolution for Men*, around which this Bible study is built. Their most recent books are *The Love Dare for Parents* and *The Love Dare for Parents Bible Study*.

Before joining Sherwood in 2001, Stephen served as a youth minister in Atlanta. He and his wife, Jill, live in Albany with their five children. Stephen is most excited about watching his kids grow up and change the world for Christ.

ALEX KENDRICK has served as associate pastor of movie outreach at Sherwood Church and cowriter and director of Sherwood's movies. In addition, he is a speaker, author, and actor—filling the roles of Grant Taylor in *FACING THE GIANTS* and Adam Mitchell in *COURAGEOUS*.

Before attending New Orleans Baptist Theological Seminary, Alex was a Christian disc jockey for two stations and a minister discipling college students in Marietta, Georgia. He and his wife, Christina, have six children and live in Albany. His proudest moments involve seeing his children make godly decisions and grow in Christian character.

TRAVIS AGNEW worked alongside Stephen and Alex in developing this study. His passion is discipling people through preaching, teaching, writing, and worship. Travis has recorded worship projects, authored books, and frequently blogs about fatherhood, family, and faith.

Travis is a worship pastor at North Side Baptist Church in Greenwood, South Carolina. Married to Amanda, he is the proud father of two sons and one daughter.

ABOUT THE STUDY

The award-winning movie *COURAGEOUS* follows law enforcement men who encounter a variety of personal, spiritual, and family challenges. A pivotal outcome of the journey for the five men was deciding *as a group* to commit themselves to God and being willing to take hard actions to be better husbands and fathers. This study unpacks biblical principles for the promises that make up the Resolution (see p. 6).

The Resolution for Men Bible Study is designed for use in a men's accountabiliy group or other short-term study. An accountability group is a small group of three to seven men who meet regularly to pray, study, and support each other in their walk of faith. Choose a schedule—weekly, semimonthly, or monthly—and a location—church, home, office, or restaurant—based on what best meets the needs of your group. A study can easily grow out of viewing the movie *COURAGEOUS,* as follow-up to *Courageous Living Bible Study* or *Honor Begins at Home,* or to jump-start your men's ministry.

Your member book is formatted into eight sessions built around the twelve promises of the Resolution. Work your way through the discussion questions in each Bible study or choose one or two questions to focus on as a group. If you desire, your group could decide to focus on one commitment per meeting, resulting in twelve sessions for study and application.

The My Resolution section allows you to personalize what you have learned from Scriptures and the group's insights. Talk together about applications and commit to pray for each other as you seek to live out your commitments. Five devotions per session further reinforce each week's focus and increase motivation.

Consider planning a Resolution Ceremony with your group after the study. And then you can take other men through this study so they can grow in Christ as well.

When a man completely resolves to live his life for Jesus Christ, his path changes, his priorities change, his passions change, his purpose changes, and his legacy changes.

Will you become a man of resolution?

THE RESOLUTION FOR MEN

The basis of what you will be unpacking with your group over the next eight weeks, the Resolution for Men expresses who you desire to be as a man and reminds you of your priceless influence on the next generation. It consists of these commitments to God and your family.

____ 1. I DO solemnly resolve before God to take full responsibility for myself, my wife, and my children.

____ 2. I WILL love them, protect them, serve them, and teach them the Word of God as the spiritual leader of my home.

____ 3. I WILL be faithful to my wife, loving and honoring her, and be willing to lay down my life for her as Jesus Christ did for me.

____ 4. I WILL bless my children and teach them to love God with all of their hearts, all of their minds, and all of their strength.

____ 5. I WILL train them to honor authority and live responsibly.

____ 6. I WILL confront evil, pursue justice, and love mercy.

____ 7. I WILL pray for others and treat them with kindness, respect, and compassion.

____ 8. I WILL work diligently to provide for the needs of my family.

____ 9. I WILL forgive those who have wronged me and reconcile with those I have wronged.

____ 10. I WILL learn from my mistakes, repent of my sins, and walk with integrity as a man answerable to God.

____ 11. I WILL seek to honor God, be faithful to His church, obey His Word, and do His will.

____ 12. I WILL courageously work with the strength God provides to fulfill this resolution for the rest of my life and for His glory.

As for me and my house, we will serve the LORD.
JOSHUA 24:15, NASB

To get a head start on this study, read the Introduction and chapters 1–3 (pp. 1–52) in *The Resolution for Men.*

SEVEN COMMITMENTS
FOR GROUP SUCCESS

All men need accountability. We need to know that others are supporting, encouraging, and praying for us as we walk faithfully before God. This is why we urge men to form Resolution Groups.

An accountability group is a small group of three to seven men with whom you meet weekly or monthly for encouragement, accountability, and prayer. A group may meet at a church, home, office, or restaurant.

Meetings should start and end in prayer, and each man should feel free to share openly and honestly in this safe circle of believers. Times of accountability should be motivated by love, and yet be firm and direct when necessary.

Be sure to allow time for everyone to have input and for expressing thanks to God for the things He is doing in men's lives. Engaging in time together outside the group can strengthen those relationships. Consider memorizing Scripture and commit to pray for each other.

Choose a leader or group member to facilitate the group each time you meet. Always keep in mind your purpose—not just to socialize but to help each other grow and live for Christ.

As your group begins this study, it is vital to agree on principles that contribute to Christian community and growing more like Christ together. Here are seven to consider and adapt for your group:

> **PRIORITY**: We will give high priority to group meetings and to the commitments we need to make, especially to God, our church, and our families.

> **PREPARATION AND PARTICIPATION**: We will participate without dominating. We will strive to come to group having read through the study material, ready to discuss it.

RESPECT: Our group will provide a safe place to share our hearts openly without fear of judgment or ridicule. Scripture teaches us to be quick to listen and slow to speak (Jas. 1:19). We will speak the truth in love (Eph. 4:15) and value one another's opinions, while allowing Scripture to help us come to godly conclusions.

CONFIDENTIALITY: In sharing thoughts and feelings related to our home, marriage, and relationship with God, we will keep all information in the strictest confidence. What happens in group time stays in group time. However, no one will be required to share.

LIFE CHANGE: The goal of any small-group experience is transformation. In each session we will identify aspects that need attention in our walk as believers, parents, spouses, and friends.

CARE AND SUPPORT: We agree to provide care and encouragement for every member, praying for each other. (Some group members may want to enlist prayer warriors not in the study, but should not reveal anything shared in confidence, positive or negative.)

ACCOUNTABILITY: We agree to let the members of the group hold us accountable to the commitments we make in whatever loving ways we decide upon. As a group, we choose to commit together to the accountability necessary to stay the course and answer the call to become men who are faithful to what we have resolved.

_____

Signed

_____

Date

SESSION 1
"I RESOLVE"

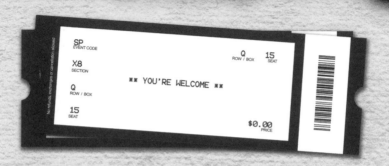

To resolve is to decide once and for all what you are living for. It's not new to today's society.

THE RESOLUTION FOR MEN

Jonathan Edwards, who preached the classic "Sinners in the Hands of an Angry God," made resolutions—70, in fact—and strived to review them once a week: "Being sensible that I am unable to do anything without God's help, I do humbly entreat him by his grace to enable me to keep these Resolutions, so far as they are agreeable to his will, for Christ's sake."

ARE YOU READY?

Meet Jay Jones, sheriff in Lee County, Opelika, Alabama. In his role, Jones courageously strives to keep his county safe—and often has to get creative with how to enforce the law.

On July 29, 2011, Sheriff Jones and his police force created a sting. Operation Iron Snare was launched to round up suspects owing more than $270,000 in unpaid child support.

Each individual received a letter saying he had won two tickets to the year's Iron Bowl game between Alabama and Auburn. The return address was the same one used in unsuccessfully trying to get them to pay child support. One by one, the suspects festively filed in to claim their tickets. Each was promptly arrested and transported to the Lee County Detention Facility.[1]

Each person who had been unwilling to show up to provide for his family willingly appeared to receive a gift of football tickets. This story reveals what we often see in human hearts: an unwillingness to resolve to do the right things.

It's time to decide and commit to be the spiritual leader in your home. To accept responsibility for your family's well-being. To make the Resolution. Maybe you are providing financially for your family, but are you providing all that *God* has required of you? Are you ready to be all that *God* has called you to be?

This Bible study will take men through all of the Resolution commitments featured in the movie COURAGEOUS and covered in depth in the book *The Resolution for Men*. We start by looking at two overarching challenges: to take full responsibility for ourselves and families and to be the spiritual leader of our home.

Commitment 1

I DO SOLEMNLY RESOLVE BEFORE GOD TO
TAKE FULL RESPONSIBILITY FOR MYSELF,
MY WIFE, AND MY CHILDREN.

Commitment 2

I WILL LOVE THEM, PROTECT THEM, SERVE
THEM, AND TEACH THEM THE WORD OF GOD
AS THE SPIRITUAL LEADER OF MY HOME.

Truth to discover: God's Word makes it very clear that the man is the spiritual leader of the home and is accountable to God for his family's well-being.

> If it is disagreeable in your sight to serve the LORD, choose
> for yourselves today whom you will serve: whether the gods
> which your fathers served which were beyond the River,
> or the gods of the Amorites in whose land you are living;
> but as for me and my house, we will serve the LORD.
> JOSHUA 24:15, NASB

TAKING RESPONSIBILITY

I DO SOLEMNLY RESOLVE BEFORE GOD TO
TAKE FULL RESPONSIBILITY FOR MYSELF,
MY WIFE, AND MY CHILDREN.

First Corinthians 13 is commonly called the love chapter. It also speaks directly to how men need to take responsibility for their home.

Read 1 Corinthians 13:4-7.

You are called to take responsibility for your family, and love is an essential ingredient to success. Read this passage again, but this time, replace the word "love" with your name. Try your hand at evaluating your success in loving your family and be ready to share with your group one area in which you would like to improve.

NOT TOO BAD

"Concerning loving my family, I'm pretty decent at being ..."

> List 1 Corinthians 13:4-7 descriptions that you do fairly well—for example, "patient" or "not boastful."
>
> 1.
>
> 2.
>
> 3.

COULD USE SOME WORK

"Concerning loving my family, I need to improve my ..."

> List actions from 1 Corinthians 13:4-7 that you still need to work on.
>
> 1.
>
> 2.
>
> 3.

> Now ask someone to read 1 Corinthians 13:11 aloud. In your mind and heart, do you truly consider yourself a man? If so, at what point in your life would you say you "became a man"?

The apostle Paul explained that part of his becoming a man was letting go of childish and immature thinking, words, and behaviors. List some immature things you stopped doing when you became a man, as well as some more mature actions you began to take as a man.

CHILDISH THINGS (What I stopped)	MANLY THINGS (What I started)
1.	1.
2.	2.
3.	3.

As a group, share your lists. As other men speak, record additional actions or behaviors that belong in each column.

What immature or childish things are you still doing that you need to let go of?

What are some things God expects from a man that you know you need to start doing?

I Will Love Them

I WILL LOVE THEM, PROTECT THEM, SERVE THEM, AND TEACH THEM THE WORD OF GOD AS THE SPIRITUAL LEADER OF MY HOME.

First Corinthians 13 calls us to love our families. God expects each man to be patient, kind, and humble. A few chapters later, Paul takes that message a step further.

> Read 1 Corinthians 16:13-14. Paul gives five instructions for men. What does each command mean in your family?
>
> 1. Be on your guard.
>
> 2. Stand firm in the faith.
>
> 3. Act like a man.
>
> 4. Be strong.
>
> 5. Let all you do be done in love.

God created men in His image. He expects us to act like men—not passive observers—loving and leading our families into a deeper relationship with Him. Even as Jesus led others by the powerful motivation of love, so God calls us to walk and lead our wives and kids with love.

Each session concludes with My Resolution pages to help you apply what you are learning. As you read these, start making plans for specific, personal commitments regarding your closest relationships. Then, each week, you will complete five days of devotions meant to help you apply the biblical principles behind them. Get deep into God's Word and deepen your resolve to be the man God has called you to be.

MY RESOLUTION

PUTTING TRUTH INTO PRACTICE

In His Word, God lays out clear expectations for us. He wants us to man up and put away childish things. He desires that we think the thoughts, speak the words, and be about the things of mature men. Knowing God's expectations is one thing; applying them is something completely different. You must get specific and practical about how you resolve to change.

In the space provided, make some personal resolves concerning the people closest to you. If you are married, your spouse gets the first spot. List your children next. Use a separate piece of paper as you need.

For each family member, take one action in each of the categories in this week's resolutions.

1. I resolve to be all that God has called me to be for _____ (name's) sake.
   - I will take responsibility for him/her by:

   - I need to do this more often because it shows him/her love:

   - I need to protect him/her from:

   - I need to serve him/her this week practically by:

   - I need to teach him/her this biblical truth:

2. I resolve to be all that God has called me to be for _____ sake.
   - I will take responsibility for him/her by:

- I need to do this more often because it shows him/her love:

- I need to protect him/her from:

- I need to serve him/her this week practically by:

- I need to teach him/her this biblical truth:

3. I resolve to be all that God has called me to be for _____ sake.
   - I will take responsibility for him/her by:

   - I need to do this more often because it shows him/her love:

   - I need to protect him/her from:

   - I need to serve him/her this week practically by:

   - I need to teach him/her this biblical truth:

DIG DEEPER THIS WEEK:
Read chapters 4–5 (pp. 54–85) in *The Resolution for Men.*

PRAYER

Take time to pray over each person on your list. Commit to putting these resolutions into practice and be open to holding one another accountable. Pray that the men in your group will be able to faithfully apply these truths in their homes this week.

Day 1

THE BLESSED MAN

PSALM 128

Every man wants a better life. While you may be somewhat pleased with things at the moment, chances are you deeply wish that they would be better. The blessing of the Lord is one of the greatest assets any man can obtain in life. But how does that happen?

> Read Psalm 128 and record the characteristics of a blessed life.

A blessed life is characterized by happiness and enjoyment of the fruit of hard work (v. 2). A blessed man's wife is vibrant and refreshing (v. 3a). His children grow and thrive (v. 3b). His legacy will benefit generations to come (vv. 5-6). All of that sounds great, doesn't it?

> What do these verses indicate is necessary to receive such a rich blessing from God?

To receive God's blessing, we must live according to God's ways. In Scripture the blessed man is known as one "who fears the LORD" and "walks in His ways" (v. 1). The man who truly honors and obeys God will be blessed.

It's simple. Fearing the Lord means greatly reverencing and respecting Him. Walking in His ways means doing exactly what He asks in the way that He asks: you love your wife the way *He* says to love her; you lead your children the way *He* says to lead them; you do your job in a way that pleases *Him*. You live to "walk worthy of the calling you have received" (Eph 4:1). If you want your life to change, to be better, then you must resolve to follow His commands.

Are you willing to do all that it takes to receive such blessing? Ask God now to make you into a man who fears the Lord and walks in His ways. Offer your commitment to God as a prayer.

Day 2

MAKING UP YOUR MIND
JOSHUA 24:14-28

God used Joshua, Moses' successor, to bring the Israelites out of the wilderness and into their long-awaited promised land. After the Israelites procured the land, Joshua delivered a final challenge. Would they follow the Lord (Yahweh) exclusively?

Joshua chose to lead as a bold preacher to combat Israel's spiritual problems. He pointed to God's past work among the Israelites. Joshua quoted the Lord's words to remind the people that every victory was His, not theirs (Josh. 24:2-13). Then Joshua drew a line in the sand.

> Read Joshua 24:14-28 and highlight phrases or verses that stand out to you.

With every ounce of his being, he would lead his family to serve the Lord. He took full responsibility for those specifically under his care. Joshua could relentlessly chase off the influence of any god but Yahweh in his own home, but he could not lead every family through the spiritual battles in their dwellings.

Have you made up your mind? Will you serve God exclusively or give Him divided attention while you serve other "gods"? While Israel faced the influences of pagan idols made of clay or stone, other issues vie for lordship in our homes: relentless pursuit of wealth and pleasure, elevation of sports or social activity above all else, and living in ways that dishonor God.

Which god will be lord of your home? Does your family know? Like the Israelites, we often are good at verbal commitments, but fall short in action. Only strong men who learn to rely on God daily will be standing and proclaiming years from now: "As for me and my house, we will serve the LORD" (Josh. 24:15, NASB).

Day 3

SHOWING YOURSELF

FIRST KINGS 2:1-4

David was anointed king of Israel at a very early age. As a young man, he killed Goliath when the bravest soldiers of the kingdom held back. He would go on to make worship of God a priority. David, in fact, was a man after God's own heart, and while he sinned greatly during his lifetime, he found his way back to God through honest repentance.

After a long life filled with ups and downs, the dying king summed up his desire for his son Solomon.

> To discover what David wished to instill in his son, read 1 Kings 2:1-4. Identify David's instructions.

David wanted Solomon to have God's best for his life. To live a life of honor, strength, and faithfulness. To stand firm in the face of temptation and do the right thing even when it was not popular or easy. Furthermore, he wanted Solomon to keep his "obligation to the LORD" (v. 3), not commit to one thing and do something else.

This father desperately wanted to know that his son would walk in the ways of the Lord. He wanted Solomon to keep God's statutes, commandments, ordinances, and decrees (v. 3).

Imagine that all of your family lived in such obedience. Can you think of a better legacy to leave than that of complete, generation-to-generation devotion to God?

Such a legacy is possible, but not just through verbal instructions on godliness. It is imperative that you live in such a way that your family cannot help but follow. Regardless of your past, pray now that God will give you the daily grace to model the way your family should live. Ask Him to make you a man who is truly found faithful to the Lord.

Day 4

FAITHFUL LOVING
FIRST PETER 3:7

Loving and leading your wife is an important part of living out your resolution. Perhaps you've never seen what it looks like for a godly man to unconditionally love his wife. Maybe you try to show your wife love but find some of your efforts met with resistance.

No matter your background or her response, you are responsible for loving the woman you married. God will not hold you responsible for what your wife says to you or how she acts toward you, but He will hold you accountable for how faithfully you love her and lead her.

> Read 1 Peter 3:7 aloud three times to internalize the truth of the apostle's instructions for the home.

What does it mean that your wife has a "weaker nature"? Does it mean she cannot lift heavy objects? Maybe. Does it mean she is more prone to cry or be emotional than you are? In some situations, yes. But this verse speaks more to the role of the husband than that of the wife.

To be stronger means that God has wired a man with extra strength to bear the greater stress, pressure, and responsibility on his shoulders. It means that in trying times, as the leader of your home, you are resolute. When the world seems to be falling apart, you are unwavering in your faith in God. Even if your bride begins to question God in a situation, you stand firm without insulting or degrading her. The apostle Peter states that if you cannot understand that your wife is a coheir of the "grace of life," your prayers themselves are hindered.

Pray now for your wife and your marriage. Ask God to give you the daily grace to lead her and your family with faith, wisdom, and strength during tough times.

Day 5

ANGRY KIDS

EPHESIANS 6:4

So many in this generation seem to have massive chips on their shoulders. Some children and teens are noticeably volatile, unable to restrain their fists or tongues. Many blame cultural influences like the media and peer pressure for their behavior.

Paul's instructions to the Romans seem to fit the claim as he describes a depraved culture (Rom. 1:24-32). In a list highlighting idolatry, homosexual sins, malicious acts, and hatred of God, Paul notes that a culture devoid of God will be characterized also by children who are "disobedient to parents" (Rom. 1:30). Interestingly, he seems to trace this condition not to the culture, but to the home.

Read Ephesians 6:4.

When fathers are harsh or hypocritical and try to correct behavior without supporting it with spiritual instruction and a good example, children grow angry. They lash out in disobedience. Temperamental fathers can actually cause further disobedience in their children.

Our kids are desperate for love and leadership. Being a dad is about much more than providing a roof over their heads and three daily meals. Successful parenting regularly shows children that nothing is more important than following God.

What are some ways your parenting makes your children joyful? Helps them know more about God? Commit to add to this list.

You can and must discipline your children, but you don't have to discipline them in such a way that pushes them away from you. Pray today that you can find out how to lead your family ever closer to God.

HONOR THE "HOLY" OF MATRIMONY

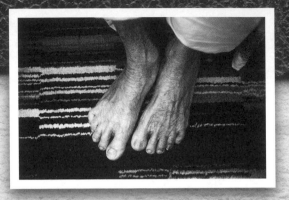

God created your marriage to be a living portrait on earth. It was designed to reveal the loving relationship of Jesus Christ with His Bride, the church—those whom He has declared "holy" unto Him (see Eph. 1:4).

Your role as the husband in marriage is to be like a giant neon sign that says, "Look at how I treat my wife! This is what the sacrificial, unconditional love of Jesus Christ for His Bride looks like!"

"A Man of My Word"

Robertson McQuilkin was living out his dreams. While president of Columbia International University, he trained and equipped ministers to serve all over the world. But when his wife, Muriel, displayed signs of Alzheimer's disease, Robertson had a choice to make. Many encouraged him to send Muriel to a nursing home because he really would not be able to help her. That way, they argued, he could continue to follow God and His calling.

But at night when McQuilkin would go home to his bride, he discovered that her bloodied feet had traveled back and forth along the road to school because she was so anxious to be near him. Choosing to love his wife and honor his vows, McQuilkin explained his decision in his resignation speech to the school:

> Muriel now, in the last couple of months, seems to be almost happy when with me, and almost never happy when not with me. In fact, she seems to feel trapped, becomes very fearful … [and is] in distress. But when I'm with her she's happy and contented, and so I must be with her at all times.

> And you see, it's not only that I promised in sickness and in health, 'till death do us part, and I'm a man of my word … It's the only fair thing.

> She sacrificed for me for forty years, to make my life possible … so if I cared for her for forty years, I'd still be in debt … It's not that I have to. It's that I get to. I love her very dearly, and you can tell it's not easy to talk about. She's a delight. And it's a great honor to care for such a wonderful person.[1]

How does Robertson's decision surprise you? How was his decision a picture of Christlike love?

How does his example challenge you as a husband?

Robertson McQuilkin did the right thing, not because he had to but because he was compelled by love for his Lord and his wife. Setting aside his own interests, he served her with gratitude and honor (Phil. 2:5). He was her delight and he chose to make her his delight.

HOLY MATRIMONY

This week's resolve commitment focuses on your wife and marriage. No matter your current marital status, God expects you to heed His instructions concerning marriage. This week will help prepare you for marriage or strengthen you as a husband.

Commitment 3

I WILL BE FAITHFUL TO MY WIFE, TO LOVE AND HONOR HER, AND BE WILLING TO LAY DOWN MY LIFE FOR HER AS JESUS CHRIST DID FOR ME.

Truth to discover: A man of resolution needs to be faithful to his wife and to lead her with Christlike love.

Marriage must be respected by all, and
the marriage bed kept undefiled,
because God will judge immoral people and adulterers.
HEBREWS 13:4

Followers of Christ are not to be like everyone else in marriage or in any other relationship: "[B]ecause it is written, 'YOU SHALL BE HOLY FOR I AM HOLY' "(1 Pet. 1:16, NASB). While many in our culture do not hold marriage in a place of honor, Christian men are called to make this commitment a lifelong priority. Faithfulness and holiness are to be the norm, not the exception.

CHRISTLIKE LOVE

"God's calling for you as a husband was not to marry the woman you love, but to love the woman you married."
THE RESOLUTION FOR MEN, PAGE 91

In Ephesians 5:25-33, Paul gives a clear example and instructions regarding what men need to do in order to have a more fulfilling and successful marriage.

> Read Ephesians 5:25-33. What is the primary command God gives to husbands in verse 25? How might your wife respond if you faithfully loved her this way?

> What do verses 26-27 show that Christ accomplished in His bride through His sacrificial love?

Do you ever find yourself waiting for your wife to become more like Christ *before* you will love her more? Or are you willing to love her fully even in her sinfulness? To make the church holy and blameless, Jesus loved her fully by *dying* for her. He gave Himself up for her.

It is with such selfless love and devotion that husbands are to love their wives, to the extent that the two become one in body, mind, and spirit (Eph. 5:28-31).

> What does verse 26 say that Jesus uses to wash and cleanse His bride?

As God does His heart work in us through His Word, the marriage commitment can bloom rather than wilt or fade. When a man loves His wife sacrificially, as Jesus loves the church, she likely will become more radiant and Christlike under his care. Arguments and anger are replaced with encouragement, respect, and devotion.

> Do you and your wife study God's Word together? What results are you experiencing individually? In your marriage?

> In verse 26 the word "sanctify" means to make holy. What does the word "holy" mean to you?

The definition of the word "holy" is "to set apart." Something becomes holy when it is set apart and made pure and special as God's own prized possession. When a man views his marriage as holy, he cherishes his wife, nourishes her with love and God's Word, and guards his marriage and wife with his life.

> Do you view your marriage as holy? How would someone else know that you do?

Are you faithful to your wife in action and in your heart?

What are some things a man can do to "sanctify" his marriage and keep it in a special place of honor?

Every aspect of marriage is to be holy. The often-used description *holy matrimony* should be a clear reminder that your relationship with your wife is to be set apart from any other relationship.

Loving your wife has nothing to do with feelings, with situations, with her responses. Love is a decision. Christ didn't "feel" like going to the cross either, but He was obedient for the joy that lay beyond it:

> Fixing our eyes on Jesus, the author and
> perfecter of faith, who for the joy set before
> Him endured the cross, despising the shame, and
> has sat down at the right hand of the throne of God.
> **HEBREWS 12:2**

The key to loving like Jesus is to understand that you cannot do it on your own. God Himself must become your never-ending Source of love (John 15:9). His Spirit is more than able to love your wife as you daily rely on Him.

1. http://www.ciu.edu/robertson-mcquilkin (accessed May 28, 2013).

MY RESOLUTION
PUTTING TRUTH INTO PRACTICE

The promise to be faithful to your wife and to love and honor her sacrificially, as Jesus loved, can help you put the truths of God's Word into practice. Don't think about how you would like love expressed to you, but what would show your wife that you love her.

Your love expressions don't have to cost money. They do, however, require some planning. Consider giving your wife at least four things throughout this study: a card, a commitment, a date, and a delightful gift. These should be unexpected and not be tied to a special day or event. Note how she received each gift and how your relationship flourished. Plan to share with your group about some of these experiences.

A Card
Give her a romantic card that communicates
how much you love her.

A Commitment
Verbally tell your wife that you are
committed to your marriage for life.

A Date
Plan out details and take her out on a date.

A Delightful Gift
Whether flowers, jewelry, or something she has specifically
requested, a thoughtful gift brings your wife joy.

DIG DEEPER THIS WEEK:
Read chapter 6 (pp. 86–99) in *The Resolution for Men*.

PRAYER

Thank God for giving you His Son. Let the attitude of Christ guide all of your relationships. Using Philippians 2:5-11, pray to worship God and seek the attitude of His Son, Jesus Christ.

Make your own attitude that of Christ Jesus, who,
existing in the form of God, did not consider equality
with God as something to be used for His own advantage.

Instead He emptied Himself by assuming the form
of a slave, taking on the likeness of men. And when
He had come as a man in His external form,
He humbled Himself by becoming obedient to the point
of death—even to death on a cross.

For this reason God highly exalted Him and gave
Him the name that is above every name, so that at
the name of Jesus every knee will bow—of those
who are in heaven and on earth and under the
earth—and every tongue should confess that Jesus
Christ is Lord, to the glory of God the Father.
PHILIPPIANS 2:5-11

Day 1

STAY CLOSE TO YOUR WIFE
SONG OF SOLOMON 5:10-16

Your wife needs your undivided attention. To focus on her properly, find out what it is about you that captures her interest.

What about you does your wife find attractive and appealing? Read Song of Solomon 5:10-16.

Did you catch that she thought her husband was "fit and strong" (v. 10)? She showered him with compliments, mentioning his head, hair, eyes, cheeks, lips, arms, body, and legs. Her husband, she felt, was eye candy! Clearly, she was enamored with him.

The wife also makes mention of something important: "His mouth is sweetness. He is absolutely desirable" (v. 16). She loved that her husband's mouth was full of sweetness. She probably wasn't referring to his kissable lips here since she had already alluded to them in verse 13. Instead, he speaks lovingly and with kindness, using affirming words that make him "absolutely desirable." This husband is the total package. He strives to be a complete, consistent man.

Don't miss the second half of verse 16: "This is my love, and this is my friend." This woman's spouse is not just her lover; he is also her friend. For a woman, these two roles go together.

Take time to really pray for your wife—not about how she can change, but about how you can better demonstrate love to her. Seek His help to faithfully keep your blessing commitments. Ask God to show you how to love her the way Jesus Christ loves. Today, in an effort to better love your wife, consider how you can be a better friend.

Day 2

FIGHT TEMPTATION
MATTHEW 5:27-30

If you've ever given blood, you have had to answer some awkward questions. Some relate to sexual activity. Even if you don't have a checkered past, answering those questions can make you really uncomfortable.

Remind yourself of the correlation Jesus sees between lust and sex by reading Matthew 5:27-30. According to this passage, when does Jesus believe that adultery takes place?

> **Based on this passage, how many sexual partners have you had in your heart over the years? Don't share your answer.**

From watching the coworker who wears revealing clothing, to online photos you may have gazed upon, to your entertainment choices, lust will lead your thoughts to sin just as serious as those that happen physically. Jesus tells us to take drastic measures: avoid lust like the plague. It destroys and creates great dissatisfaction. It makes us angry and discontent with God's blessings.

> **Read Job 31:1. What do you think it means to make a covenant with your eyes?**

Many men—including Christians—struggle with the temptation to view pornography. If you need support in battling this issue, read pages 244–247 in *The Resolution for Men* and be willing to take radical steps to get this addictive poison completely out of your life.

Day 3

CONSIDER THE CONSEQUENCES

2 SAMUEL 12:7-15

Scripture describes David as a man after God's heart. As a passionate worshiper, brave warrior, and decisive king, David was used by God to change the landscape of Israel. While many of his victories brought his nation great triumph, his personal downfalls caused great pain. Had he paused to consider the consequences of his actions, his family would have been spared devastating fallout.

Maybe you remember the situation that tarnished David's walk of faith. When King David should have been in battle, he relaxed in the comforts of his palace. A stroll along the roof line led him to see a beautiful woman bathing. David sent someone to bring her to him; the king slept with her and then quietly sent her home. Weeks later, Bathsheba informed the king of her pregnancy: the baby was clearly his.

The woman's husband, Uriah, was fighting on the battlefield. David called him home, attempting to cover up the incident by allowing Uriah some time with his wife. But out of loyalty to his fellow soldiers, Uriah denied himself the privilege. David, possibly hoping to avoid scandal, had Uriah killed on the battlefield. Risking his own life, the prophet Nathan confronted and rebuked King David.

> **Read 2 Samuel 12:7-15 for the outcomes David's actions set in motion. What consequences do affairs bring today?**

Adultery always brings consequences. David's family was never the same. Yours won't survive unscathed either. Proverbs 6:27-29 warns: "Can a man embrace fire and his clothes not be burned? Can a man walk on burning coals without scorching his feet? So it is with the one who sleeps with another man's wife; no one who touches her will go unpunished." (See *The Resolution for Men*, pages 231–232, for ten potential consequences of adultery.)

Day 4

DIVORCE IS NOT AN OPTION
MATTHEW 19:1-9

Marriage should be entered into with a one-way-ticket mentality. Unlike a vacation when you find out along the way that you don't like the accommodations and decide to turn back, marriage is meant to last from "I do" until death. No two-way tickets should be considered; yet, many enter into marriage thinking that a spouse remains on a trial basis and can be dismissed when necessary.

Regardless of your mistakes in the past, you must resolve for the future that divorce is not an option for your marriage. Take the very word out of your vocabulary.

Does the Bible make allowances for divorce? While the Bible does permit divorce in some situations, Scripture never advocates it.

> **Read Matthew 19:1-9. For what reason did Jesus say divorce was permissible?**
>
> **How would you describe the way Jesus feels about divorce in any instance?**

Giving a wife a certificate of divorce in Old Testament times was a better alternative than some actions taken by men who had grown weary of their wives. Jesus pointed out that God allowed the practice because of the hardness of people's hearts, but that He desires a husband and wife not to separate. The grace of God can revolutionize any marriage, and He can resurrect any marriage if the couple will just die to themselves.

Maybe you have biblical grounds for divorce. You might be ready to call it quits in your marriage. But will you do the difficult thing? Will you work at your marriage? Will you remove divorce as a possibility? Decide today to fight for your marriage and to strengthen the relationship with your bride. You can, with God's help.

Day 5

PURSUE YOUR WIFE EXCLUSIVELY
FIRST CORINTHIANS 7:1-5

Men love the prospect of a new car. But have you ever noticed that after seeing the new models, your own car doesn't seem to cut it anymore? Amidst many options, the model you own suddenly seems dissatisfying.

Men tend to fantasize about the prospect of being with another woman. Whether the temptation comes virtually or physically, a man who feasts his eyes on a "newer model" can begin to think his wife no longer measures up.

The solution to your sexual desires is to nurture and find fulfillment in the gift you already have. In fact, the best way to avoid sexual temptation is to have better sex with your wife more often. First Corinthians 7:1-5 is a passage worth reading!

In this passage Paul responds to a situation in the Corinthian church. Since sexual sins were so rampant, some thought it would be best for a Christian to avoid sex completely. Paul, however, was mindful that sex is a gift from God. He reminds people of God's design, instructing the people that they should have sex with their spouses.

What instructions does Paul give those who are married?

Every man has sexual desires, and God created a plan for fulfilling them. Don't cheapen God's gift with a lustful thought or pornographic image or by considering the merits of another woman.

Instead, choose to completely love and serve your wife. Make her the singular focus of your romantic pursuit. Choose to pursue sexual satisfaction with only your spouse. Go on a mission to win her heart and become an honorable man at home, and your wife will begin to desire you more intimately. You will be amazed at all the ways God will bless you when you decide to do just that.

NEVER TOO LATE TO CHANGE

Praise the LORD! How blessed is
the man who fears the LORD,
Who greatly delights in His commandments.
His descendants will be mighty on earth;
The generation of the upright will be blessed.
PSALM 112:1-2, NASB

SMALL GESTURE, HUGE IMPACT

Thomas was a "good enough" dad. He stayed faithful to his wife, provided for his family, never committed any "really bad" sins, and took his children to church. But something was missing from his life.

In his late 60s, Thomas was exposed to biblical teaching about a father's responsibility to teach biblical truths to his children. Through the conviction of God's Word, Thomas began to seek out exactly how God had called him to live. Then, when he saw the movie COURAGEOUS, he realized that being a "good enough" dad would not leave the legacy he wanted.

At first Thomas thought it was too late. His children were on their own, married with their own children. While they were fine members of society, they were keeping God as part of their homes, not the centerpiece. They were repeating a pattern of behavior they had seen since childhood.

One day Thomas decided it was not too late to be the kind of father God expects. He gathered his grown kids together and apologized for not being all that God had required of him. Then he asked them to begin watching his life to see how his new commitment to the Lord was changing him.

That small gesture had a huge impact. Thomas began calling his sons to share Scripture and prayers for them. He began taking his grandchildren on fishing outings, telling them stories about Jesus. He began to change his interactions with his wife until everyone could see she was more joyful.

Over time, Thomas's family learned from his example. Generations of his family are now different because of his resolve to begin living out his love for the Lord.

What is the best advice about parenting you were given before becoming a father?

If you could change anything about your parenting, what would it be?

This week, two commitments direct our focus to what God expects of fathers in their responsibility for their children.

Commitment 4

I WILL BLESS MY CHILDREN AND TEACH THEM TO LOVE GOD WITH ALL OF THEIR HEARTS, ALL OF THEIR MINDS, AND ALL OF THEIR STRENGTH.

Commitment 5

I WILL TRAIN THEM TO HONOR AUTHORITY AND LIVE RESPONSIBLY.

Truth to discover: A father is primarily responsible for the spiritual growth, training, and well-being of his children.

> Remember also your Creator in the days of your youth. ...
> Fear God and keep his commandments,
> for this is the whole duty of man.
> ECCLESIASTES 12:1,13, ESV

LIKE FATHER, LIKE SON

I WILL BLESS MY CHILDREN AND TEACH THEM TO LOVE GOD WITH ALL OF THEIR HEARTS, ALL OF THEIR MINDS, AND ALL OF THEIR STRENGTH.

Children don't just physically resemble their families. They often develop habits similar to those of their parents or siblings.

> Which of your traits or habits would you like your children to have? How have your spiritual habits and faith impacted the faith of your children?

> Someone read aloud Deuteronomy 6:4-9. What specific applications do these verses encourage fathers to make?

It is God's will that we love Him, obey Him, and live for Him. He should always be our greatest priority and first love. But this is also how we are to define success for our children and grandchildren.

> How do you think your children would describe your personal love for God?

Fathers must first have a love for God in their heart before they can teach or model love for God to their family.

> How can you help your children love God with all of their heart? With all of their mind? With all of their strength?

Such modeling is part of your daily interactions—as you greet your kids at the breakfast table, have spiritually rich conversations in the car, or pray together each night. Instilling a love for God in your children is one of the most important things you could ever do.

TRAINING CHILDREN

I WILL TRAIN THEM TO HONOR AUTHORITY AND LIVE RESPONSIBLY.

Training children to honor authority and to live responsibly is another way to ensure that they live godly, productive, purposeful lives. It starts with their attitudes toward their parents.

> **Read Ephesians 6:1-4. Whom does Paul say children are to obey? To honor?**

Paul wanted children to be respectful of all authority, but especially of their parents. The Greek word for "obey" used in verse 1, *hypakouō*, means to submit to in light of the person's authority. Children are to obey even if they do not agree. The Greek word *timaō*, for "honor" in the verse that follows, means to estimate the value of, to revere. Children are to esteem their parents because it is right in God's eyes and because parents are responsible to Him as their caretakers.

> **Who does Paul say is responsible for training children?**

While both parents are to instruct and disciple their children to love and obey God, Paul clearly sets the father as the one to take the lead.

> **What did Paul tell fathers *not* to do?**

What are some ways fathers exasperate their children?

If you spot any of the following "heart hindrances" in your relationship with your children, be willing to apologize, quickly get to the heart of the matter, and pray about how amends might be made.

- No time at home
- Anger
- Unjust discipline
- Hypocrisy
- Lack of compassion
- Favoring one sibling over another
- Unrealistic expectations
- Hurting their mom
- Misunderstandings

But how do we help our kids take messages of authority, respect, and godliness to heart? Discipling kids requires discipline.

What do you better understand now about how your parents disciplined you?

Read Hebrews 12:5-11 aloud. What does this passage assume every father will do? For what purpose (v. 11)?

Discipline helps our children realize that sin is not only dishonoring to God and dishonoring to us, it also is harmful to them. The opportunity to share in the very holiness of God is at stake (Heb. 12:10).

As the Book of Proverbs and Deuteronomy 30 reiterate, the right choice is the smart one (the path to blessing), and the wrong choice is the stupid one (the path to punishment). And discipline is what brings this point home for kids. It gives a clear, negative connotation to sin's costly consequences. When you train your children to honor, respect, and obey you, you are also preparing them to honor, respect, and obey God, their Heavenly Father.

My Resolution
PUTTING TRUTH INTO PRACTICE

1. Read John 15:9: "Just as the Father has loved Me, I have also loved you; abide in My love" (NASB). The way you express love to your children is influenced by how your father expressed love to you.

> How did your dad do with showing you love? Circle your choice. He hit a:
>
> GRAND SLAM
>
> HOME RUN
>
> BASE HIT
>
> STRIKEOUT
>
> Now, how do you think your kids would score you regarding how loving you are to them?
>
>
> What needs to change so that they will more deeply feel your love?

2. If you were remodeling a house, you would take a systematic approach to your work. You would determine which room needed the most attention and start there first. You would gather and organize tools for the job and call in professionals when needed. Planning and intentionality are just as important in guiding your children.

Try summarizing your goal for your children in the same way.

I earnestly desire that my children:

The area needing the most attention in my home is:

The most significant need for change in my home is:

To better help my children to love and obey God in the future, I need to:

In what areas do you need some training? Someone else's help? Who or what kind of help can you seek?

My next three steps will be:

DIG DEEPER THIS WEEK:
Read chapters 7–8 (pp. 100–129) in *The Resolution for Men*.

PRAYER

Pray over what God is revealing to you and commit to teach your children to love Him above all else and to honor His authority.

Day 1

GIVING YOUR CHILDREN ATTENTION
MALACHI 4:6

It's impossible to teach your children anything if you don't first have their attention. Often, however, they withhold their attention until they are sure they have yours.

Think through the last few weeks, months, or year. When did your children last have your full focus? Describe the occasion and be sure to include where you were and what you talked about.

Interestingly, the last verse of the Old Testament speaks to fathers giving their children attention. As Malachi eagerly awaited the Messiah's arrival, he shared that something critical would take place shortly before His coming.

Read Malachi 4:6. What does it mean for a father's heart to turn to his children?

Your children need you to be involved in their lives. They are blessed by your provision and may well enjoy the attention of a mother who gives them hours of one-on-one care, but that does not replace their need for quality time with you. Giving them that focus and attention may require you to set aside the TV remote or the work you are doing at home.

Malachi revealed that when fathers' hearts turn toward their children, then children's hearts turn to their fathers. Pray that God will help you turn your heart toward your children and help them turn their heart toward you.

Day 2

Giving Your Children Affirmation
MARK 1:9-11

We all have defining moments in our lives. Think for a moment. What was the most meaningful or hurtful thing your father ever said to you? (If you didn't have a relationship with your biological father, choose another close relationship when you were growing up—your stepdad, a coach, a mentor, etc.)

The words you just recalled were spoken decades ago, but you still remember how they made you feel, how they impacted you as a child. Our words have great power.

How often do you use the power of words to affirm your children? Do you freely praise them?

Kids need and are blessed by affirmation. Our Heavenly Father supplied a powerful example of how a parent should affirm the son or daughter he delights in. On the day Jesus was baptized, His Father spoke some words that would make any child beam.

Read Mark 1:9-11. What did God say about His Son?

Notice that while God spoke these words to His Son, He did so in a place where others could hear Him. God was filled with joy about His Son, and He wanted everyone to know it! Have you ever communicated similar words of affirmation to your children? Pray that God will help you to do so in the days ahead.

Day 3

GIVING YOUR CHILDREN AFFECTION
DEUTERONOMY 1:30-31

Like a father about to take his children into an expensive store or restaurant, Moses rallied the family together for one final talk. He used this time to remind them of God's commands with a "Deuteronomy" (which means a "second telling" of the Law).

> **Read Deuteronomy 1:30-31 to see how Moses described God's actions toward His people. To what did Moses compare God?**

This description reveals a lot about how God cares for us. Just as important, it tells us a lot about what God expects from fathers. Moses noted that a father will carry his son in the wilderness, thus protecting him from the sun and relieving his tired feet. In difficult traveling conditions, the father chooses to bear pain and weariness rather than to overwhelm or exhaust his young boy.

Similarly, an affectionate father sometimes stoops to pick up his tired child as they travel through life's wilderness seasons together. He allows his child to find security, comfort, and rest at his expense. Secure and comfortable, a child cannot think of a better place to be.

You may not naturally be an affectionate man. You may not have received a lot of physical touch from your parents. However, what we don't receive may be the very thing we go looking for elsewhere.

In the next few days, we challenge you to provide loving arms and affectionate touches for your children to reassure them of your love. Be willing to hold them or let them cry. Don't hesitate to offer that hug or reassuring pat on the back they need.

Day 4

RESPECTING AUTHORITY
ROMANS 13:1-7

In addition to training your children to submit to your authority, you are also responsible for teaching them to honor other authorities. *The Resolution for Men* suggests some questions to ask to determine the kind of example you are setting:

- When you're at home, how do you talk about your leaders at work and church?

- What do your children hear you saying about elected representatives? Even when you disagree with them, are you respectful?

- Do your children see you praying for people who are in authority over you (1 Tim. 2:1-4)?

- How do they see you respond to speed limits, red lights, and police?

- Do your actions match your talk about how God places authorities in our lives for our benefit?

> Read Romans 13:1-7. How does God expect us to behave toward the authorities in place over us? Who set those authorities in place?

While our authorities are imperfect, we must remember that a perfect God has established them for our good and has commanded us to honor them out of our honor of Him. God has placed authorities over our lives for a reason and a purpose.

Day 5

RIGHTLY CORRECTING BEHAVIOR

PROVERBS 29:15-17; 13:24

We live in a culture that greatly disagrees over how children are to be disciplined. However, discipline is a private matter between parents, their children, and God. As Christians, we are wise to follow the words of Scripture. There we find solutions based not on theory but on truth.

> **Read Proverbs 29:15-17. What disciplinary action does the Bible endorse?**

Does the Bible encourage spanking? Yes, as a form of loving training. Never abuse. Does it ever encourage parents to vent uncontrolled anger on children? Absolutely not. In fact, the Bible warns fathers not to stir their children up to anger (Eph. 6:4) and is clear that we should treat others as we would like to be treated. By rightly and firmly correcting bad behavior, a parent can know he has done everything in his power to keep a child from disgrace.

Many people in our culture use the phrase "Spare the rod, spoil the child" without knowing its origin. The concept developed long ago.

> **Write out Proverbs 13:24.**

God's Word says that if you don't "use the rod," then you hate your child! Why? Because if rebellious children go unchallenged, they grow into adults who rebel against employers, officials, and even God. The act of spanking, then, might actually save their lives as they are lovingly forced to recognize that there is someone else in control in this world!

Passive parenting may receive endorsements elsewhere, but the Bible is clear that if you love your children, you will discipline them.

FIGHT FOR WHAT IS RIGHT

Defend the cause of the weak and fatherless;
maintain the rights of the poor and
oppressed. Rescue the weak and needy;
deliver them from the hand of the wicked.

PSALM 82:3-4, NIV

Feed the hungry and help those in trouble. Then
your light will shine out from the darkness, and the
darkness around you will be as bright as noon.

ISAIAH 58:10, NLT

BURDENED BY GOD

Randy was nearing retirement when he became burdened for a cause he had never before considered. His children were out of the home, he had served his church faithfully, and he eagerly awaited the payoff of hitting the golf course every day. Everywhere he turned, though, he became increasingly aware of a big problem.

The world is filled with orphans.

Some boys and girls were orphaned because their parents became ill and died. Some became orphans due to their still-living parents' selfish neglect. Randy really wanted to see someone do something about this huge problem.

"But, honestly," he later admitted, "I didn't want to be the one."

In spite of his initial reservations, Randy found himself burdened by God to help address the issue. The more he learned about the state of the world, the further he dove into Scripture in hopes of finding answers. He was amazed to read about God's care for orphans and the responsibility of God's people in making sure their needs are met.

Amidst his concerns over his age, finances, and abilities, Randy began to act. At a very "undesirable time," Randy decided to do something to correct an injustice.

Randy became a father again. And again. And again. At last count, Randy had adopted seven children, some of whom had been abused in an international system. Some were unable to receive the medical care they needed. All were in desperate need of a father's love to calm the chaos in their lives.

Instead of being discouraged by the needs around him, Randy decided to put his faith into action. He has never regretted it.

For what reasons do you think Randy initially balked at the idea of adoption?

What do you think changed his mind?

It's easy to become overwhelmed with the needs of the world. While we may talk about society's needs in general terms, pray about them, or give money to help, the man of resolution will see what he can do about making the world a better place. Part of answering God's call to be a godly, faithful man means stepping up to make a difference:

> ## Commitment 6
>
> I WILL CONFRONT EVIL, PURSUE
> JUSTICE, AND LOVE MERCY.

Truth to discover: Every generation needs strong men to rise up courageously to confront evil and injustice.

> Mankind, He has told you what is good
> and what it is the LORD requires of you:
> to act justly, to love faithfulness,
> and to walk humbly with your God.
> MICAH 6:8

Anytime a man gets serious about loving God and loving his neighbor, it will always lead him out of his comfort zone. It will move him to a place where he has to get his hands dirty meeting needs and extending mercy, while bringing about justice and confronting evils that oppress the helpless and downtrodden.

FIGHT FOR WHAT IS RIGHT

Missionaries like John Wesley and Charles Finney actively opposed slavery. Evangelist D. L. Moody opened a home to rescue girls from exploitation. Pastor Charles Spurgeon built homes to help elderly women and orphans in London. Each was a Christian man who responded to local problems regardless of opposition. Their lives were powerful because they lived and practiced the gospel they believed.

Confront Evil—Scripture records the stories of many men who took a stand to confront evil. Let's learn from their examples.

When the prophet Nathan heard about King David's adulterous relationship with Bathsheba, what did he do about it (2 Sam. 12:7-9)?

When Nehemiah heard that God's people were taking financial advantage of others, what did he do about it (Neh. 5:6-13)?

What did Jesus do when He encountered men corruptly profiting in God's house (Matt. 21:12-13)?

What commonality do these men share?

Pursue Justice—"The recent church history in America includes a lot of good men doing nothing. Men who are wired, called, and empowered to be men of action, yet who choose to be soft, insensitive, and passive—men who fail to remember that 'to one who knows the right thing to do and does not do it, to him it is sin' (Jas. 4:17, NASB). Passivity is a curse" (*The Resolution for Men*, p. 137). Men of resolution courageously pursue justice. If injustice exists, men of God rise up to confront it.

Read Micah 6:8.

Scripture makes clear our responsibility. God's Word tells us what is good. He has told us what He requires.

Describe our three responsibilities as presented in the Micah verse. Then explain what each requirement means to you. Share your answers with your group.

1.

2.

3.

Working with someone else, describe five injustices in the world today—whether in your town or on the other side of the planet. Which ones most need to be fixed?

1.

2.

3.

4.

5.

If you know of ministries in your church or community that actively fight these injustices, identify them.

Love Mercy—As men of God who have been changed by the mercy of God, we should extend mercy to others. Of course, we want people to experience the spiritual mercy found in a relationship with Christ, but we must also want them to receive mercy in practical ways.

> Read Matthew 25:31-46.

According to Christ, in what situations do people need mercy?

1.

2.

3.

4.

5.

6.

According to this passage, whom are we actually serving when we meet practical needs?

MY RESOLUTION
PUTTING TRUTH INTO PRACTICE

Our world has many needs. You cannot do something about all of them, but you can do something about some of them. You can spend your life confronting evil, pursuing justice, and loving mercy. Your life can change other people's lives.

Certain needs mentioned throughout this session probably resonated more with you than others. Every person is wired differently—that's part of the beauty of the body of Christ! God designed you to get involved in meeting a specific need about which you are passionate.

> What problems or causes grabbed your heart when growing up?

> Consider family or friends who have experienced some type of enslavement, addiction, or injustice. Which of these situations most grieved you?

> Of all the needs discussed in this lesson, which do you expect will most haunt your thoughts this week? Why?

Do you see commonalities in your answers to these questions? Does one topic make your heart beat faster than the others? If so, define it here:

Why do you think this cause means so much to you?

What ministries or groups are already active in helping with this cause? How could you use your time and energy to do something about this situation?

DIG DEEPER THIS WEEK:
Read chapter 9 (pp. 130–143) in *The Resolution for Men*.

PRAYER

Pray for the people impacted by the circumstance that most fuels your compassion. Pray that you will not settle into sympathy for them, but rather that passion will mobilize you to help. Commit to partnering with God to do something about the situation and share this commitment with your group.

Day 1

THE SIN OF OMISSION

JAMES 4:17

If you were brought up in church, you may have been warned to abstain from certain "top sins." As a result of such lists, religion is often perceived as a "thou shall not" way of living.

> **List five sins you were taught to avoid.**

Did you know that there are also sins of omission? That we sin by failing to do certain things? Read James 4:15-17 to find out more.

James reminds us that we must be careful how we live and plan our lives accordingly. He then states that "it is a sin for the person who knows to do what is good and doesn't do it" (v. 17). To better understand sins of omission, also read James 2:15-17.

The Bible makes it clear that if we know something ought to be done, corrected, or addressed, and we stand idly by, we commit just as serious a sin as we do when we commit a wrong against God or someone else.

Take a moment and ask God to reveal some areas that need addressing in your home, community, or church.

> **What do you feel God is leading you to do about these issues? Commit these actions to God and ask Him to continue to lead you.**

Day 2

WHOSE APPROVAL DO YOU SEEK?

GALATIANS 1:10

We pray that the Holy Spirit is directing your heart toward a cause for which you will fight. As you start to put feet to the idea on your heart, you might experience pushback from people who won't understand your determination to follow God.

In those moments, you must decide, *Whom will I please? Will I seek the approval of man or the approval of God?* Read Galatians 1:10 for the apostle Paul's take on this issue.

Paul called it right: each person will either spend his life seeking the approval of men or the approval of God. You cannot have both.

> What conflict might you face as you take up the cause God is laying on your heart?

> Who might try to pull you off course?

> What would it look like to please people in this situation? To please God?

No doubt about it, the resolve to courageously fight for a cause will create opposition. Determine to keep your eyes focused on seeking the approval of God rather than the approval of man. Pray that God would give you the grace to let go of the fear of man and to embrace a greater respect and love for God.

Day 3

GREATER IS HE

FIRST JOHN 4:4

Jesus stated that our enemy, Satan, comes "to steal and to kill and to destroy" (John 10:10). He wants to completely undermine your fight. As you try to unite your family to join you in your cause, you may find the enemy trying to distract you or steal your joy. If you try to mobilize the men in your church to lead, he likely will attempt to discourage them from helping.

Should you try to seek justice for people in unfortunate situations, the enemy will set his efforts toward destroying your progress. Satan always attacks where God is working and lies to us that our efforts are in vain. While his attack might be brutal, Satan has met his match in Jesus Christ, your defender and champion.

Read 1 John 4:4.

If Jesus Christ is your Lord and Savior, then you find your identity and purpose in Him. If He gives you specific guidance on something He wants you to do, the Lord will give you all that you need to see it through. You act as His ambassador, and you don't have to fear the enemy or walk in defeat. Why? Because "the One who is in you is greater than the one who is in the world' (1 John 4:4). Jesus has already disarmed the power of the enemy through His cross (Col. 2:13-15).

Do you truly believe God can handle *everything* that opposes you?

If you currently face opposition, journal your thoughts about it. Ask God to help you trust Him as He capably handles the situation in His perfect timing.

Day 4

LOVE YOUR NEIGHBOR

LUKE 10:25-37

Someone who has truly experienced mercy will much more freely show mercy. It becomes a habit. Whether in the form of forgiveness or meeting a physical need, every follower of Christ is commanded to love his neighbors. But who exactly qualifies as a neighbor?

   Read Luke 10:25-37.

To answer this question, Jesus shared the parable of the Good Samaritan. When Jesus first told the story, He likely shocked and offended many people within earshot.

   Why? When Jesus mentioned a priest and a Levite walking by a man in great need, He depicted the most religious people of the day as compassionless and unconcerned. The Samaritan, the one who went out of his way to generously meet the needs of the injured man, was an outcast of Jewish society. By His actions, however, he proved to be the most devoted to showing compassion and love to his fellow man.

   Who might Jesus use today in place of the priest and Levite? The Samaritan?

   Based upon your recent actions in addressing people's needs, with which character do you most identify? Why?

Pray now that God will give you the heart of the Good Samaritan so that you will allow yourself to be inconvenienced to reach out to others in need.

Day 5

PROVIDE JUSTICE

PSALM 82:3-4

While God cares for the needs of the many who need to be evangelized, fed, adopted, or rescued, He also cares for each needy person by name.

> It's time to get specific. Read Psalm 82:3-4. Record the name of someone who might fit in each of these categories. Indicate an action you could take to help.

Who is needy?   What could you do for them?

Who is fatherless?   What could you do for them?

Who is oppressed?   What could you do for them?

Who is destitute?   What could you do for them?

Who is poor?   What could you do for them?

Did your understanding of who is needy, fatherless, and oppressed change when you put a name to each need? In Psalm 82, originally a worship song, God reminded His people to seek justice and make right the tragic things of this world.

God desires that we step into situations and do something about the unfortunate circumstances of others. He wants us to reach out in love, to see the people behind those needs as the precious individuals for whom He sent His Son to die.

Pray that God will give you the compassion of Christ and open up your busy schedule so you can reach out to someone in need.

ETERNAL INVESTMENTS PAY OFF

A man resolves one day but then must live it out
and keep recommitting to it every day after that.
THE RESOLUTION FOR MEN

For this reason, ever since I heard about your
faith in the Lord Jesus and your love for all
God's people, I have not stopped giving thanks
for you, remembering you in my prayers.
EPHESIANS 1:15-16, NIV

A Legacy of Love

Evangelist Rick Via has shared the gospel in more than 40 countries. While Rick has been very active in the church throughout this time, his greatest contribution to the kingdom comes in a different arena.

Rick and his wife, Janet, have five grown children who are all involved in some type of ministry. They are blessed to have an ever-growing number of biological and adopted grandchildren. While he has made contributions to countless lives around the world, Rick never stopped investing in his children.

Over the years as Rick watched his children marry, he had the privilege to share at their rehearsal dinners how he had prayed for each child and his or her future spouse. He noted how God had faithfully honored those prayers:

> For years I have prayed what I would call general prayers for my children ... for their health, safety, behavior, and studies. I have always also prayed prayers focused on specific situations and events concerning their mates, college, life's calling, seminary, place of ministry.

> We always know we are praying in the will of God when we pray Scripture over our children. I would usually choose New Testament epistles, using verses that speak of character and godliness. I have also prayed against such things as alcohol and drug usage, profanity, ungodly associations, and unhealthy relationships.[1]

While Rick has done much through his life as a minister, his legacy is multiplied in the lives of his children who are benefiting from his love, devotion, and prayers. If Rick had solely focused on his ministry, his children would have missed out on so much that he could have offered them.

How has Rick's ministry been multiplied through his investment in his children?

We need to pray for those who are closest to us and treat them with Christ's love, a timely challenge expressed in this commitment:

Commitment 7

I WILL PRAY FOR OTHERS AND TREAT THEM WITH KINDNESS, RESPECT, AND COMPASSION.

Truth to discover: Justice and truth must always be balanced with kindness, respect, and compassion.

> Therefore, God's chosen ones,
> holy and loved, put on heartfelt compassion,
> kindness, humility, gentleness, and patience.
> COLOSSIANS 3:12

MAN OF PRAYER

Who taught you how to pray? How did they teach you?

While Jesus was on earth, His disciples constantly saw God's power at work around and through His life. They watched Jesus feed 5,000 men with only a handful of food, heal every type of disease, and walk on water. When they watched how He acted, they noticed how dependent He was on His Heavenly Father. These men could have asked the Lord anything, but wanted to know more about this relationship.

Read Luke 11:1. What did the disciples want Jesus to teach them to do?

The disciples knew that when Jesus prayed, great things happened! Read aloud Matthew 6:9-13 for Jesus' complete answer to His followers.

Dissect this prayer as if it were your first time to hear it. Using your own Bible, write out each phrase. Then rewrite each phrase in your own words, noting the different topics Jesus taught us to include in our prayers. Share some answers with your group.

Verse 9:

Verse 10:

Verse 11:

Verse 12:

Verse 13a:

Verse 13b:

By His example and instructions about prayer, Jesus taught us to:
1. address God as our Father while honoring Him as holy;

2. prioritize His kingdom while submitting to follow His will;

3. rely on Him as our source of provision to meet all our needs;

4. daily confess our sins while freely forgiving others;

5. ask for His help in avoiding internal sins and in being delivered from Satan's external attacks; and

6. praise Him as the Owner, Sovereign, and Worthy God of the universe.

What a great model Christ has given us to help become powerful men of prayer. When you pray, remember each phrase of His Model Prayer to pray more strategically for your family and others around you.

DEMONSTRATING LOVE

Read Colossians 3:12 (p. 68) aloud as a group. Identify the characteristics God expects us to demonstrate.

To be a man of resolution, you must commit to demonstrate Christ's love to all people. By showing kindness, respect, and compassion, you represent Jesus to a world desperately in need of His love. Displaying these attitudes doesn't make you a pushover. Jesus Christ was the toughest man to walk this earth but also the most compassionate.

Sometimes, showing kindness to people means doing or saying the hard thing. "But that's love. That's caring more about what someone else needs than about what they want or whether they like you or not. Most men don't have the guts to do this. Demonstrating love often means doing something hard and uncomfortable if it's what's best for a friend" (*The Resolution for Men*, p. 153).

> How would your behavior be different at home if your daily responses were packed full of compassion, kindness, and patience?

> Think of someone you know who is straying from God. If you did for him only what he wants you to do, what action would you take? How would your words or actions change if you were driven by love to do what he needs?

How we pray and the way we treat others are two of the most important aspects of our lives as Christian men. And these two go together. We will not treat others with lovingkindness or patience if we are not relying on God in prayer each day.

Plugging into the vine of close fellowship with Christ will empower you to walk in love and bear much spiritual fruit. A man who stays in God's Word daily and cries out to Him in prayer will develop discernment, greater love for his wife and children, and the grace to resist temptation. We must stay close to Him!

As a group, pray that God will make you into mighty men of prayer and that He will fill you with His love for those around you. Ask Him to help you to daily clothe yourselves with the kindness, respect, and compassion of Christ.

1. Rick Via World Reach Ministries 2011 [cited January 2012]. Available from the Internet: *http://rickvia.org/about/about-us/*

My Resolution
PUTTING TRUTH INTO PRACTICE

"As for me, I vow that I will not sin against
the LORD by ceasing to pray for you. I will
teach you the good and right way."
1 SAMUEL 12:23

The thought that we sin when we fail to pray for people is convicting. Godly men seek to grow more like Christ in every way possible. Use Matthew 6:9-13 as a guide to pray for yourself and others.

HONOR GOD (V. 9)
For what reasons will you honor God today? Think about who He is and what He has done. Get specific.

COMMIT TO FOLLOW GOD'S WILL (V. 10)
What do you need to do to follow God's will?

Do you know someone who needs you to pray that he or she would obey God's will? Explain.

DEPEND ON HIS PROVISION (VV. 11-12)
What needs should you put in God's hands?

Consider the people who are closest to you. For what needs of theirs should you pray?

CONFESS SIN AND FORGIVE OTHERS (V. 12)

What sins do you need to confess to God today?
Whom do you need to forgive? Why?

Does anyone close to you need to forgive someone?
How should you pray?

ASK FOR HIS DELIVERANCE AND HELP IN OVERCOMING TEMPTATION (V. 13A)

For what temptation do you need God's help? For whom
do you need to pray to resist temptation?

Pray for God's ongoing deliverance from any evil or harm
that the enemy would try to inflict on you or your family.

PRAISE HIM (V. 13B)

Praise God by using names or adjectives that describe
Him. Thank Him for being so many things to you.

DIG DEEPER THIS WEEK:

Read chapter 10 (pp. 144–55) in *The Resolution for Men* and The Locks
and Keys of Effective Prayer (pp. 122–123 in this book).

PRAYER

You have identified plenty of needs. Now, get to work! Get on your
knees, talk with your Heavenly Father, and pray for one another.

Day 1

GET INTENTIONAL IN PRAYER
MATTHEW 6:7-8

This week's devotions are meant to help you improve your prayer life. You will look at some of the locks or barriers that make prayers ineffective, as well as at some keys that enable us to pray effectively. (See pp. 122–123 in this book, The Locks and Keys of Effective Prayer.)

Our prayers are ineffective when we pray repetitive, empty words, thinking God is pleased with our excessive speaking. To better understand what this means, read Matthew 6:7-8. Jesus didn't say "If you pray" but "*When* you pray" (italics added). He assumes believers will pray.

> **What do you think Jesus meant when He said, "Don't babble like the idolaters"? What would that look like today? What is the danger of praying "many words"?**

Prayer should be an intentional, coherent, worshipful conversation with God. Prayer should characterize our life and be about quality, not ritual. Most likely, your kids are learning to pray from you. Do they repeat a simple rhyme over a meal? Could you finish their sentences when they pray? Or is it conversational? Do they take time in prayer, thanking God for His blessings and humbly asking for His help?

There are so many ways to keep prayers fresh and engaging. First, consider the current needs, worries, and opportunities before your family. Get intentional about praying together about these issues. Add variety and passion and intentionally work to improve how your family prays. Most of all, pray together. Perhaps choose a different prayer focus every day. (Sunday: situations around you; Monday: missionaries; Tuesday: tasks; Wednesday: work; etc. Or come up with your own.)

Day 2

PRAY WITH RIGHT MOTIVES

JAMES 4:3

Children have a way of expressing humanity's sinful tendencies. Young children share toys to get their own way. Older children act out of self-ishness rather than love. Teenagers become sneaky about Internet use or manipulative in order to get their own way.

Grown-ups play a similar game as we ask for help meant not to glorify God but to feed our selfish impulses. Instead of begging God to act for the glory of His kingdom, we implore that He move to benefit our desires and personal kingdoms. This affects our prayer lives.

Read James 4:3 and describe the included warning.

James warns believers that certain prayers will not be answered. Regardless of how eloquent or passionate the pleas, prayers spoken from sinful motives will not be granted. God wants to give us the good things we request (Matt. 7:11), but not the idols of our heart.

The reality is, only God knows the pureness of your heart (Jer. 17:9-10). It's one thing to pray for your spouse to repent and another to pray that she gets struck by lightning. It could be good to pray for a better job to provide for your family, but not for winnings to come from poker games. The motives behind prayer should never be sinful.

For what have you recently asked God?

How will God be glorified if your prayers are answered? Will you honor Him if He grants your request?

Day 3

PRAY IN SECRET
MATTHEW 6:6

Jesus instructed His followers to pray privately, to God who is "in secret" with us when we pray.

> Read Matthew 6:6. What does Jesus promise if we follow this instruction? What do you think that means?

Corporate prayer will always be an important aspect of faith. There is something special about a member of God's people standing up and praying so the rest of the congregation can engage and join in. While this type of prayer has its place, Jesus wants believers to experience prayer that is heard only by God.

> Read Matthew 6:1 to discover why.

When we offer prayers meant to impress others, God is not impressed. In fact, if you offer religious service to impress people, you lose your reward from God (Matt. 6:1). Check your motives this way:

I pray more when I am ☐ alone. ☐ around others.
I worship more when I am ☐ alone. ☐ around others.
I study the Bible more when I am ☐ alone. ☐ around others.

Take some time to pray—really pray—in secret.

Day 4

Prayer and Fasting
ACTS 14:19-23

Scripture is full of instructions and examples of fasting and yet the practice is often absent in churches. Fasting is a way to intentionally deny ourselves something we usually enjoy in order to focus our attention on seeking the Lord (Isa. 58:6-10). In her effort to rescue the Israelites, Esther asked all of Israel to fast (Esth. 4:16). Before launching His focused period of ministry, Jesus fasted for 40 days (Matt. 4:1-11). And in His teachings, Jesus identified benefits of fasting (Matt. 6:16-18).

> **How many times have you intentionally fasted to seek the Lord?**

> **What prevents you from fasting more often?**

As the early church began to gain momentum, Christ-followers had to make critical decisions as they made disciples and established new churches. Read about a specific encounter as it relates to fasting.

> **Summarize the events of Acts 14:19-23. Why do you think the disciples included fasting in their activity?**

When you fast, you deprive yourself of food, pleasure, or entertainment for a period of consecration and focus. Fasting tells God that you desire His will more than your comfort. Each time your stomach growls or your head throbs, you can accept it as a gracious call back to prayer. You show God how serious you are about seeking Him when you fast.

   If a burden lies heavy on your heart or you desire to see God move in a certain way, plan a day of fasting. Commit this opportunity to God and put it on the calendar.

Day 5

Abiding in Christ

JOHN 15:5-7

The press secretary for the president of the United States must be prepared to speak on behalf of the president. The only way to confidently speak for the one in charge is to spend time with the leader, aware of his agenda and knowledgeable about how he would answer questions.

Wouldn't it be great if you spent so much time with God that you knew how He would respond to whatever question life threw your way? Your time in His Word and in listening to Him through prayer will teach you just how He would respond.

Read John 15:5-7.

It is impossible to do anything without Jesus. We are dependent on Him for our very life. As we abide, or remain in close fellowship with Jesus, He gives us a staggering promise: "If you remain in Me and My words remain in you, ask whatever you want and it will be done for you" (John 15:7).

I can have whatever I want? Of course you can, because as you walk with Christ, He changes your desires to line up with His. You can trust all the promises in the Word of God. As you daily walk with Him, you will begin to seek His will and heart in all situations.

You treasure His Word so much that you read it because you cannot help yourself. You memorize His words because you cannot think of any greater words to speak. As you set your mind on things that will reach people for Christ and advance His kingdom on earth, then you can ask for whatever you want and watch God answer in amazing ways.

1 2 3 4 **5** 6 7 8 9 **10**

On a scale of 1 to 10, how well do you abide in Christ?

HUMBLY PROVIDE

A resolution is not a promise of perfection;
it is a commitment to a direction.
THE RESOLUTION FOR MEN

In the Old Testament, Joshua resolved, "As for me and my
house, we will serve the Lord" (Josh. 24:15, NASB). King David
set this direction: "I will give heed to the blameless way. I will
walk within my house in the integrity of my heart. I will set no
worthless thing before my eyes; ... He who walks in a blameless
way is the one who will minister to me" (Psalm 101:2,3,6, NASB).

Serving with Honor

Jonathan never pictured himself as unemployed. He held a bachelor's degree and even a master's; he felt that the combination would make him a great candidate for many jobs. After working during school, Jonathan received a great job with a good salary and benefits.

After a few years in his job, however, Jonathan took a stand that cost him in the eyes of his employers. Unwilling to back down from his convictions, Jonathan was forced out of his job. He sent out resumes all over town, knowing that he couldn't look for unemployment outside the city because of his family's needs. But all of his job hunting led to nothing.

Finally, Jonathan found a job. Unfortunately, its requirements were beneath his education level and the salary didn't compare to his prior compensation. Most daunting was that the role left him vulnerable in the public eye.

He had to choose: would he humbly provide for his family or remain unemployed to protect his reputation as a businessman? Jonathan resolved to provide. He knew it was his calling.

One day, Jonathan's former employer walked into the establishment where he worked. While a rush of humiliation initially washed over Jonathan, he served the man with dignity.

When Jonathan went home that night, the awkward encounter was forgotten in light of his family's joyful reception. He realized that while his reputation in certain circles might have been tarnished, his reputation at home and in heaven remained strong in the eyes of God.

How would most men in Jonathan's situation respond?

Explain the difficulty of following Jonathan's example.

Read Proverbs 13:4; 14:23.

> The slacker craves, yet has nothing,
> but the diligent is fully satisfied. ...
> There is profit in all hard work,
> but endless talk leads only to poverty.
>
> PROVERBS 13:4; 14:23

What will the hard worker gain according to both verses?
What will the slacker receive?

In this session, you will take a very practical look at providing for your family. Your resolve to provide will guide that process.

Commitment 8

I WILL WORK DILIGENTLY TO PROVIDE
FOR THE NEEDS OF MY FAMILY.

Truth to discover: Men should consider it an honor to embrace their role as the primary providers of their families.

THE BREADWINNER

Work is a gift, not a curse. But because of the curse, men have to work harder in life. Part of God's expectation is that we work hard to provide for the needs of our families. The man of the house is expected to be the primary breadwinner.

Look up the following passages, noting God's specific expectations for men. In some cases you will discover a specific trait or attitude He expects from His followers. Write a short phrase explaining what each passage teaches you about work and provision.

- Genesis 3:17-19

- Proverbs 10:4

- Matthew 6:25-34

- Ephesians 6:5-7

- 2 Thessalonians 3:7-10

- 1 Timothy 5:8

- 1 Timothy 6:8

When we get prayerfully busy trying to provide for our families, we find ourselves cooperating with the One who created it all, owns it all, and can make more of it whenever He wants. By laying our best before Him, we can be absolutely sure that He will "give us each day our daily bread" (Matt. 6:11). He is *Jehovah-jireh*—the God who provides.

WHAT A FAMILY NEEDS

The difference between wants and needs is often blurred. For many of us, our standard of living is so subjective that we no longer are certain what qualifies as necessary for survival.

Write out the words to Philippians 4:13.

This Bible verse is frequently quoted. Unfortunately, it is sometimes applied to situations for which it was not intended.

Now read Philippians 4:10-14.

[10]I rejoiced in the Lord greatly that once again you renewed your care for me. You were, in fact, concerned about me but lacked the opportunity to show it. [11]I don't say this out of need, for I have learned to be content in whatever circumstances I am. [12]I know both how to have a little, and I know how to have a lot. In any and all circumstances I have learned the secret of being content—whether well fed or hungry, whether in abundance or in need. [13]I am able to do all things through Him who strengthens me. [14]Still, you did well by sharing with me in my hardship.

Now verse 13 takes on a different meaning, doesn't it? The apostle Paul didn't mean to convey that you can do whatever you want through Christ's strength—including working constantly to gain all your wants. Instead, Paul meant that through Christ's strength, we can be content in all circumstances, finding satisfaction in God's faithful provision. Paul "learned" how to do this (v. 11). It may not have come naturally.

Now record the different ways Paul said we should be content in verses 11-12. Once you have done that, highlight the word "all" in verse 12. Then draw arrows from that word to all that it describes.

In which situation do you struggle most to be content?

Your family needs to recognize the sufficiency of Christ and to understand the difference between wants and needs. As the family leader, part of providing is to help them make this distinction. More important, you must be content before you can lead your family to experience the attitude of contentment.

So, what is it that your family needs financially? Physically? Emotionally? Spiritually?

You should avoid thinking that financial provision is the extent of your responsibility as a husband and father. Bringing home a paycheck and keeping your family clothed and fed are not where provision stops. As the shepherd-leader of your home, you are also responsible for providing spiritual and emotional sustenance for your family to feed on—and you provide the example they look toward.

Whether or not they show it or say so, your family depends on you. God has gifted you and allowed you to partner with Him to provide for all their needs, including their spiritual and emotional well being. At the same time, God will give you joy and a sense of fulfillment as you step up and provide for those He has called you to love the most.

Have you resolved in your heart that you will work diligently in the days ahead and be a strong provider for your family?

MY RESOLUTION
PUTTING TRUTH INTO PRACTICE

Providing for your family presents one of those interesting paradigms in God's kingdom. In some ways, you are to do all that you possibly can to provide for your wife and children. On the other hand, you also are to pray and believe that God is your Source and will be the One who provides all that you need to fulfill your responsibiities. Accepting that which "our hands have done" is a gift and a reminder that the Lord offers us a wonderful partnership and privileged responsibility.

> Think through how you and your family are doing.
> Use these questions to gauge the strength of your
> commitment to work with God to provide for them.

- What needs in your immediate family are not being met? What can you do to help? Are you praying about this need?

- What needs would your wife say that you are not meeting as you should?

- Are there widows in your extended family who struggle financially or who need day-to-day assistance such as lawn mowing? How can you help? How should you pray for this person?

- If you have children, would you characterize them as selfish or selfless? What attitudes in your home might be contributing to their mind-set?

Sometimes children who have been given a lot are unable to cope with the work that is required when they launch out on their own. Consider helping your children thin out their toys or clothes, donating the objects to a charity or others in need.

Assuming they are old enough, your children can begin to work for an allowance and learn financial responsibility. Share and use basic budgeting principles that reflect biblical stewardship and godly gratitude.

What are you doing to model a strong work ethic for your children?

How can you help protect your wife from carrying a heavy financial strain?

Does she desire to be a homemaker? If so, are you working toward allowing her to do so? (Titus 2:5).

DIG DEEPER THIS WEEK:
Read chapter 11 (pp. 156–167) in *The Resolution for Men*.

PRAYER

List action steps you need to take and prayers you need to pray concerning how to provide for your family. Commit your plans into God's hands and wait to see what He will do for you and through you to help meet the needs of those under your care.

Day 1

WORSE THAN AN UNBELIEVER
FIRST TIMOTHY 5:8

"Blessed are the breadwinners. As men, we should consider it an honor to embrace our role as the primary providers of our families. This is part of our manhood and calling as representatives of God the Father—the One who established work as part of His creation and is *still* 'working' (John 5:17) as an example for us to follow, continually providing for our daily needs" (*The Resolution for Men*, p. 157).

Whether you love your job or hate it, God desires that you embrace the opportunity to provide for your family through your vocation. Unfortunately, many men find themselves unemployed and unable to provide. Many reasons exist for this problem: economic turndowns, physical handicaps, and poor work attitudes or work ethic.

If sinful behavior such as laziness or disrespect of your superiors contributed to your being unemployed, repent before God and eagerly seek new work. If you became unemployed due to circumstances beyond your control, ask God for His help and relentlessly pursue job opportunities great or small to provide for your family and honor God in the workplace. Be willing to work at lower paying jobs until you can find a higher paying one.

Read 1 Timothy 5:8.

Paul's words are scathing. To call someone who does not provide for his family worse than an unbeliever is a serious charge. The implication is that a man of God will not allow his family to go without basics. Through prayer, active pursuit of new jobs, and a willingness to work in even humbling circumstances, a man of God will not rest until his family's needs are met. Be willing to do what it takes to provide. Humility and a determination to take the opportunities God sends your way set an example that will change your family forever.

Day 2

MAKE MORE TO GIVE MORE
EPHESIANS 4:28

Money is a tool. In and of itself, money is not evil but can be used for good or bad. The love of money, however, is the root of all types of evil (1 Tim. 6:10). However, earning money is actually a good thing.

Read Ephesians 4:28.

In this verse Paul refers to a man who used to take advantage of others for financial gain. But when the thief was changed by the power of God in his life, Paul expected him to stop his thievery and get to work. Why? To make money—income that would not only lessen the desire to steal but would help to meet the needs of others. In Christ, we should see opportunities to *make* more as opportunities to *give* more.

Why do we strive to make more money? To buy more? To give more?

While it is acceptable to spend money on a home, a hobby, or an investment, it is not acceptable to drain your resources on things that only benefit you. Whether in your church, community, or neighborhood, you will hear about financial needs. People who experience hard times need resources to put food on their tables and to heat their homes. Those who are called to full-time ministry may require funds they don't have in order to keep sharing the gospel in a distant land.

Men, it is our responsibility to avoid hoarding our income. We should be ready and willing to bless others with our overflow.

Are you aware of a financial need around you? What can you do to help?

Day 3

NEVER FORSAKEN

PSALM 37:25-29

"Men work. Men provide. And when those men are children of God who call on Him as their Father, they can be sure that God will always meet their needs" (*The Resolution for Men*, p. 160). Sometimes, though, even the hardest working man endures financial challenges. Families grow, bills increase, companies downsize, unexpected expenses occur, and salaries change. The wise man remembers that in all these circumstances, God provides.

> Read Psalm 37:25-29. What things does the righteous man do? What does God do?

When you dedicate your life to Him, God doesn't promise that He will meet all your wants; but He does promise to meet all your needs in Christ Jesus (Phil. 4:19). When men live God's way, the favor of God rests on them, and He will take care of their needs and their families. If you are under financial strain, pray for God's provision, continue to work hard, and trust that God will meet every need.

> Does any financial strain weigh on you now? If so, describe it.

Give it to God right now in prayer and trust that He will provide for those who are right with Him.

Day 4

HURRYING AFTER WEALTH
PROVERBS 28:21-22

While making money is not a sin and can certainly help you be open-handed in assisting others, it is important to recognize that an overly ambitious heart can lead to greed and the downfall of your integrity.

> **Describe what each verse warns about wealth:**
> **Proverbs 11:28**
>
> **Proverbs 23:4**
>
> **Proverbs 28:6**
>
> **Proverbs 28:22**
>
> **Ecclesiastes 5:10-12**

Proverbs 28:22 tells us that the "greedy man is in a hurry for wealth; he doesn't know that poverty will come to him." Don't shortcut your way to financial prosperity; you might lose your integrity along the way. Or, sadly, you may discover that the security you worked so hard to build has vanished like smoke.

Don't live in a desperate attempt to get more. Work hard, stay faithful, and trust that God will give you every dollar needed to cover your costs while also helping others.

Day 5

LEARNING CONTENTMENT
FIRST TIMOTHY 6:6-10

Have you ever had this experience on Christmas morning? Your child tears open one gift to behold something he has desperately anticipated. Then, before the wrapping paper has had time to fall to the floor, he is already reaching for the next shiny package.

You may acknowledge the blessings you have. You probably even give thanks to God for them. But sometimes discontent sets in.

> **Read 1 Timothy 6:6-10. According to the apostle Paul, what are our two physical needs (v. 8)?**

Have you eaten today? Do you have clothes to wear? Jesus explained that God will always supply these two things to His children (Matt. 6). But are you content? Really content?

As you fall into wishing you had someone else's house, a larger bank balance, or more of a certain item, beware: "those who want to be rich fall into temptation, a trap, and many foolish and harmful desires, which plunge people into ruin and destruction" (v. 9). Dissatisfaction with your blessings can lead to ruin and destruction.

Choose contentment. Today thank God for your food, clothing, and the very air you breathe. Look for and express gratitude for the many blessings He constantly pours out on you and your family.

Regardless of how much we have, we can allow greed to cause us to set our heart upon gaining more, or we can let gratefulness flow out of us in joyful thanksgiving to God for what He's already provided. What will you do?

FORGIVE AND BE FORGIVEN

Judge not, and you shall not be judged.
Condemn not, and you shall not be condemned.
Forgive, and you will be forgiven.

LUKE 6:37, NKJV

If you want to see a happy person, look at someone who has just
been forgiven! But there's another joy worth pursuing—the liberation
you feel after forgiving someone who has deeply hurt you. When
wounded people finally forgive, the dark clouds part in their emotions,
and a breath of fresh air and sunshine rushes into their hearts.

THE RESOLUTION FOR MEN

CONTAGIOUS GRACE

Andy grew up in a single-parent home. Estranged from his father for most of his life, he grew up hating this shadow of a man of whom he had only heard rumors. The more he heard, the angrier he became.

Instead of trying to exact revenge, Andy was more clever. He desired to be successful in the hope that his father would hear about his son's success and feel sadness and regret. His goal was to pay his father back by showing that he had never really needed him in the first place.

Then Jesus changed that. Andy was saved by the love of Christ. God continually worked on his character. Andy began to read the Bible and start applying what was in there until he reached the sections about forgiveness. "Just as the Lord has forgiven you, so you must also forgive" (Col. 3:13b). He knew that God was calling him to forgive his father—and was scared to death.

After days of prayer and fasting, Andy searched online to find his father's phone number. His attempts to talk himself out of calling were too late when his father picked up the phone. Through sheer willpower, Andy uttered the words to a voice he did not know: "This is your son, Andy. I'm not calling to yell at you or ask for something. I'm calling to tell you that Jesus Christ has forgiven me and, regardless of how much hurt you have caused me in this life, I forgive you. I will never hold anything you have done to me against you ever again."

Long story short, these two generations are finding out more and more about the grace of Jesus. Andy's father once said, "This grace thing is contagious. I held in so much bitterness toward others who had hurt me. Once Andy forgave me, the hurts I held over others' heads seemed so trivial and I began forgiving them as well."

What do people generally seem unwilling to forgive? How would you compare those issues to the challenge Andy faced?

Forgiveness is a defining characteristic of Christianity—we receive it from Christ and offer it to others. God wants Christian men to become masters of forgiveness and reconciliation.

Commitment 9

I WILL FORGIVE THOSE WHO HAVE WRONGED ME AND RECONCILE WITH THOSE I HAVE WRONGED.

Commitment 10

I WILL LEARN FROM MY MISTAKES, REPENT OF MY SINS, AND WALK WITH INTEGRITY AS A MAN ANSWERABLE TO GOD.

Truth to discover: Freedom from regret and sin is God's gift to us through the death and resurrection of Jesus Christ. But we do not enjoy or walk in this freedom until we willingly forgive others.

> "For if you forgive men their trespasses, your heavenly Father will also forgive you. But if you do not forgive men their trespasses, neither will your Father forgive your trespasses."
> MATTHEW 6:14-15, NKJV

> "So if you are offering your gift on the altar, and there you remember that your brother has something against you, leave your gift there in front of the altar. First go and be reconciled with your brother, and then come and offer your gift."
> MATTHEW 5:23-24

MOVING ON

I WILL FORGIVE THOSE WHO HAVE WRONGED ME
AND RECONCILE WITH THOSE I HAVE WRONGED.

Everyone will be hurt and wronged many times throughout their lives. The question is whether we will continue to forgive as Jesus commanded. At times, this week's subject will seem intense. Know that in this group you have freedom to share with brothers who will care for you along the way.

Why is it so hard to forgive those who have hurt us?

Read Colossians 3:12-15 aloud. Who set the standard for how we should forgive others (v. 13)? How many of your sins did He forgive?

Every sin is against God, but what exactly has He done to wrong you?

If He was willing to sacrifice His own Son to forgive you, what are you willing to give up in order to forgive others?

Most relationships involve scars from wrongs committed by both parties. The unique thing about our relationship with Jesus is we are 100 percent the problem. He never does anything to strain the relationship between us, and He never provokes us to do evil. We do all the damage on our own.

Yet God still forgives us. Completely. He doesn't make us pay Him back for His Son's death on the cross. He doesn't remind us of our mistakes. He didn't even wait for us to fix them before offering us a relationship.

Christ's example is our model. We are to forgive the way He forgave us. But often our approach to forgiveness is very different from His.

Contrast our common expressions with God's attitude.

MY ATTITUDE	GOD'S ATTITUDE
"I can forgive, but I can't forget."	Jeremiah 31:34:
"But they don't deserve my forgiveness."	Romans 5:8:
"I may forgive him, but I don't want to be around him."	Ephesians 2:3-6:
"I'll forgive her, but she doesn't need to know about it."	Hebrews 12:14-15:

We must commit to forgive others just as Jesus forgave us. Muster the courage to look deeply into yourself and your motives and relationships. Is there even one person you have not fully forgiven for what he or she has done to you? That is one too many. Are you grateful for God's forgiveness? Will you not extend His grace and fully forgive others from your heart?

I WILL LEARN FROM MY MISTAKES, REPENT
OF MY SINS, AND WALK WITH INTEGRITY
AS A MAN ANSWERABLE TO GOD.

Only when we resolve to reconcile with our past are we able to walk with integrity as men answerable to God. When our mistakes hurt others, God expects us to take the needed steps to make things right.

Read Matthew 5:23-24. Why is reconciliation is so critical?

The Scriptures in this session teach similar responses when you have been wronged and when you have wronged someone. In both cases, God holds someone responsible to make it right: you! You are to do your part in bringing about full reconciliation.

What keeps most men from making amends when they hurt someone? What does God think about this excuse?

Integrity reflects God. There is no deceit in Him. And because He is looking for followers who will worship Him "in spirit and truth" (John 4:24), your role as a man of resolution is to embrace a life of truth and integrity before Him. When you do, He promises these rewards:

- Blessings in your heart, the light of a clear conscience, the confidence of knowing you don't have to be afraid of bad news or being found out (Ps. 37:37; 112:7).

- Blessings in your home—"The one who lives with integrity is righteous; his children who come after him will be happy" (Prov. 20:7).

- Blessings in your city—the influence of your dependability and honesty on the entire community around you (Prov. 11:11).

My Resolution
PUTTING TRUTH INTO PRACTICE

It's time to show Christ's power through your life and let go of all the baggage. Reconciliation is both beautiful and liberating. For those who have wronged you, take time to pray and say the words, "I forgive them" to God from your heart. For those you have wronged, ask God to coordinate your paths so you can ask for their forgiveness.

Develop an action plan to honor God by requesting or offering forgiveness in the following situations.

Situation 1
Name of person I've wronged or who has wronged me:

What happened:

Why I haven't reconciled up to this point:

Specific step I can take today to extend or seek forgiveness in honor of what Christ did for me:

Situation 2
Name of person I've wronged or who has wronged me:

What happened:

Why I haven't reconciled up to this point:

Specific step I can take today to extend or receive forgiveness in honor of what Christ did for me:

Situation 3
Name of person I've wronged or who has wronged me:

What happened:

Why I haven't reconciled up to this point:

Specific step I can take today to extend or seek forgiveness in honor of what Christ did for me:

DIG DEEPER THIS WEEK:
Read chapters 12–13 (pp. 168–195) in *The Resolution for Men.*

PRAYER

Thank Jesus for His complete forgiveness in your life. Commit to show that grace to others or request that grace from others as often as is needed. Ask God to help you find the words to say. Enlist accountability from other godly men as you move forward.

Day 1

LET IT GO

ROMANS 12:17-21

When wronged, it's easy to turn into judge, jury, and executioner. If you've been unfairly hurt, it seems fitting to take a little vengeance and even the score. The problem is, setting things right is God's job, not yours. You can forgive "the same way Jesus forgives: freely and willingly [as you] acknowledge God as the rightful Judge over that person's life" (*The Resolution for Men*, p. 176). Romans 12:17-21 sheds light on how God wants us to handle our hurts.

> Who do you still need to forgive? (Record a name or initials.) The person who hurt you deserves what kind of punishment, according to verse 17?

Our flesh seeks justice to be served by our hands in a way that benefits us, ignoring the concept of mercy. But God's Word tells us we should do our part to be at peace with everyone—even those who hurt us.

> What can you do to live at peace with the person you identified earlier, according to verse 19?

> Why would God ask you to repay harm with good? What good could you do to the person who has harmed you?

Commit to loving the Lord this week by demonstrating kindness and forgiveness to the person who has hurt or wronged you. Hand over the situation to God's capable hands and do your part to live at peace. It's time to let that hurt go.

Day 2

THE ART OF RECONCILIATION
MATTHEW 5:23-24

Who has a problem with you? Maybe she has said things to you or about you. Maybe he has failed to keep up his end of the deal. The issue that stands between the two of you is so powerful that you sense the conflict when the person's name is mentioned. Today, no matter what you have on your agenda, let reconciliation take priority.

Read Matthew 5:23-24.

Jesus taught that if you know someone who has something against you, then you are responsible for fixing it. It's normal for you to think that if someone has something against you, he or she should be the one to patch things up. But Jesus calls us to uncommon love and logic.

If someone doesn't like you, do what you can to change things. If someone has problems with you, do whatever you can to make peace (Rom. 12:18) and do it right away. Even if you are in the middle of worship and remember the tension, Jesus would be pleased if you walked out of the service and took care of business.

Who has a problem with you? Define it.

How can you address the situation? When will you address it?

If you didn't answer that last question with "right away," scratch out your response and replace it with "immediately." Obey Christ. Put reconciliation into motion.

Day 3

LEARN FROM YOUR MISTAKES
PROVERBS 26:11

"A wise man learns quickly from his errors and adjusts his path to get back on track. He tries to *fail forward*, becoming wiser after each mistake and taking intentional steps to avoid stumbling into the same ditch twice. A foolish man, however, *fails backward*, refusing to learn, continually wasting his experiences. He follows his own footprints into yesterday's traps and gets entangled in them all over again" (*The Resolution for Men*, p. 183–84).

No one is perfect. In fact, even the godliest people are far from it. The truth is, you will not stop messing up until you reach heaven. So in the meantime, are you failing forward or failing backward? Are you learning from your mistakes or playing the fool?

Proverbs 26:11 vividly describes the situation of someone who cannot learn from his mess-ups. To let this verse resonate, fill in the key words from your own Bible translation:

Like a _____ returns to its _____

so a _____ repeats his _____ .

The act of repeating a mistake should be repellent. Whether your sin is of the mind, mouth, or hand, it should break your heart. Your love for Christ and His Word should be so intense that the very thought of falling into the same temptation twice should turn your stomach. And yet, if we repeat a sin after repenting, it shows that we never really thought it all that vile in the first place.

If you find yourself repeating the same mistakes and getting caught in a cycle of sin, ask God to make you disgusted with the things that disgust Him. Get radical about cutting off the things that keep leading you into a ditch.

Day 4

SILENT SINS

PSALM 32:3-4

While our sins are against God (Ps. 51:4), they have a way of negatively affecting others. We must address the sin in our lives.

> Read Psalm 32:3-4. What are the effects of silent sin, according to these verses? What happened to the psalmist when God's hand was heavy upon him?

The psalmist was burdened by the weight of his sin as God pressed him to repent. Once he confessed his wrong before God, he found release from shame and guilt (v. 5).

> Read verses 1-5 to get the full picture. What word best describes the man whose sin is forgiven?

The man whose sin is forgiven is joyful. No longer riddled with shame and guilt, the forgiven man lives in joyful abandon because of the grace found in God. Does a secret sin wear you down? Do you need to confess something to God? To your wife? To your accountability partner? To the guys in your group?

If you find yourself wasting away with shame, it's time to get some relief. "Therefore, confess your sins to one another and pray for one another, so that you may be healed. The urgent request of a righteous person is very powerful in its effect" (Jas. 5:16). You don't have to tell every detail of what happened, but you will benefit from the support and prayers of trusted friends. Confess *everything* to God; forgiveness, healing, and joy await.

> What is your action plan today to find peace?

Day 5

WALK WITH INTEGRITY

MATTHEW 15:1-9

Hypocrisy. It happens when hands raised in praise are also being used for sin. It occurs when lips proclaiming the Lord are likely to spew insults. It happens every time a man's reputation differs from his character. In the Bible the Pharisees were condemned for their hypocrisy. But are we so very different? Read Jesus' words in Matthew 15:1-9.

Jesus condemned the Pharisees and scribes because they were more concerned about people breaking their traditions than keeping God's commandments. They were infuriated that Jesus' disciples did not follow protocol when it came to washing their hands before eating. Their irritation had little to do with hygiene and a lot to do with their desire to control others and appear holy, not by seeking God but by following a strict set of rules.

Jesus was exhausted from their unwillingness to see the big picture. "These people honor Me with their lips," the Lord noted, "but their heart is far from Me" (v. 8)—hypocrisy. Men of resolution must walk with integrity and honor God as we do what His Word says. That means being the same man in secret as we are in church.

How do you think other people view your commitment to God by the ways you speak and act? Rate yourself.

1 2 3 4 5 6 7 8 9 10

They don't know
I'm a Christian.

They know I authentically
love and serve Him.

How would your wife and children answer this question? Commit to walk with integrity as your heart, mouth, and actions match the reality that you are a man who belongs to Jesus Christ.

"I RESOLVE..." FOR A LIFETIME

If He is for us, it doesn't matter who
or what is against us. We are here on
this earth at this moment to be like His
Son, Jesus Christ. We are here to boldly
speak the words, do the work, and carry
out the will of our Father. Regardless
of what our culture says, regardless of
what other men do ... for the sake of the
generations that will come after us.

THE RESOLUTION FOR MEN

"Do Good, Son"

From behind the pulpit, Mark McMinn pulled out his cell phone and held it up for the congregation to listen. The occasion? His father's funeral.

Mark's father, a pastor, had died a few days earlier in a car accident. Out of the cell phone came a voicemail message Phil had left his son just days before the tragedy. The message held the last words Mark would ever hear his father speak.

Phil's voice came in loud and clear, moving many people to tears. It was the kind of message a father might leave his son if he knew he was about to die; but in this case, of course, Phil had no idea.

> Hey, I just wanted you to know I was sorry I couldn't spend more time with you tonight. I was really missing you, and just wish I had had more time to sit down and visit with you.
>
> I love you an awful lot. I pray for you. I believe God is going to do great things in your life, man. And I look forward to maybe spending some more time with you on Friday, I'll see you later.
>
> Do good, Mark, do good. I'll see you later.

Mark explained that this was the kind of message he regularly received from his father. His dad wasn't calling to tell his son something he needed to do. He wasn't checking on Mark to make sure he was doing well in classes.

Phil McMinn called his son for the sole purpose of telling him he loved him. He wanted his boy to know he was proud of him. He adored being Mark's father.

What do you find most powerful about Phil's message?

Would you want messages you leave for your family to be broadcast at your funeral? Why or why not?

For the past seven weeks, we have studied Resolution challenges and commitments God is calling us to make as men of faith. For the last week, we want to highlight the final two commitments:

Commitment 11

I WILL SEEK TO HONOR GOD, BE FAITHFUL TO HIS CHURCH, OBEY HIS WORD, AND DO HIS WILL.

Commitment 12

I WILL COURAGEOUSLY WORK WITH THE STRENGTH GOD PROVIDES TO FULFILL THIS RESOLUTION FOR THE REST OF MY LIFE AND FOR HIS GLORY.

Truth to discover: A man's greatest goals are faithfulness and a godly legacy.

God, create a clean heart for me and renew
a steadfast spirit within me.
PSALM 51:10

Therefore, my dear brothers, be steadfast, immovable,
always excelling in the Lord's work, knowing
that your labor in the Lord is not in vain.
1 CORINTHIANS 15:58

A MAN OF GOD

I WILL SEEK TO HONOR GOD, BE FAITHFUL TO HIS
CHURCH, OBEY HIS WORD, AND DO HIS WILL.

The prophet Nathan had confronted David in his sin. Many men in David's position would have gone on the defensive and fought back, perhaps even ordering the prophet killed. After his adulterous relationship with Bathsheba and attempted cover-up by murdering her husband Uriah, David was sinking fast morally—yet recognized that the grace of God was still available.

Under deep conviction by the Holy Spirit, David repented and sought restoration, acknowledging his sin and who he had sinned against. Psalm 51 is the worship song David wrote out of his brokenness and gratitude for God's grace and mercy.

> Read Psalm 51:1-13. Record five phrases that hold meaning for you.
>
> 1.
>
> 2.
>
> 3.
>
> 4.
>
> 5.
>
> Read Psalm 51:6-13 aloud. What would it mean to have a "steadfast spirit" (v. 10) in your relationship with God? In your relationship with your family?

The people in our lives deserve consistency. Sin takes us off track and makes us inconsistent in our walk and words of faith. We must pray that God will renew within us a steadfast spirit—unwavering and purposeful—to obey His will fully.

> **What would it mean to be steadfast in your relationship with your church?**

When you got connected to Christ, you also became spiritually connected to everyone else who is in Christ. "We, who are many, are one body in Christ, and individually members of another" (Rom. 12:5, NASB). We are permanently joined together and deeply need each other.

Whether you are married or single—if Jesus is your Lord, the church is your spiritual family. Being faithful, loving the church, sharing your life with others is part of His plan for you. Let this study be an occasion to recommit yourself to your local church family.

ALL OF MY DAYS

I WILL COURAGEOUSLY WORK WITH THE STRENGTH
GOD PROVIDES TO FULFILL THIS RESOLUTION
FOR THE REST OF MY LIFE AND FOR HIS GLORY.

A Bible study should be more than an educational course. The truths you learn as you dig into God's Word should last a lifetime, changing the way you relate to God and to other people. (See Jas. 1:22-25.)

Please avoid making shallow commitments to follow Christ. Instead, walk daily in His truth and commit to be faithful for the long haul.

As a disciple of Jesus', the apostle Peter reveals a lot about the struggle to live as a consistent Christian. Let's learn from him.

> **What do you learn about words and actions from these verses?**
> **Matthew 16:16,22**
>
>
> **Matthew 26:35,69-74**

Peter's commitments were shortlived. He said one thing and then allowed circumstances to change his actions. He would proclaim undying loyalty to Jesus; then, when following Him was difficult, he fled.

At times, perhaps your story is like Peter's or David's. You exemplify great faithfulness and courage alongside valleys of failure and inconsistency. Our gracious God is more concerned with what you do from this point forward than with what you have done in the past.

> **Read Acts 4:13,19-20. What do you learn about Peter and about God's Spirit here?**

Don't obsess over past mistakes. Ask Him to fill you with His Spirit and to strengthen you to do the right thing in the future. God's Spirit is the engine that empowers our heart to live the Christian life. He makes a major difference in every aspect of our life as we submit to Christ daily.

MY RESOLUTION
PUTTING TRUTH INTO PRACTICE

We have covered a lot of biblical truth in this study. You may feel overwhelmed by the expectations God has for you as a man of resolution. That's good! You must rely on Him for your strength. This is not a one-day sprint; it is a long-range marathon of learning to live courageously for Christ one step at a time.

Remember the Lord's words to Joshua: "Haven't I commanded you: be strong and courageous? Don't be afraid or discouraged, for the LORD your God is with you wherever you go" (Josh. 1:9).

Let's review the Resolution commitments you have already made. Look back at page 6 and at previous sessions to include your action steps.

SESSION 1 (PP. 9–22):
What commitments did you make that you need to apply?

SESSION 2 (PP. 23–36):
What commitments did you make that you need to apply?

SESSION 3 (PP. 37–50):
What commitments did you make that you need to apply?

SESSION 4 (PP. 51–64):
What commitments did you make that you need to apply?

SESSION 5 (PP. 65–78):

What commitments did you make that you need to apply?

SESSION 6 (PP. 79–92):

What commitments did you make that you need to apply?

SESSION 7 (PP. 93–106):

What commitments did you make that you need to apply?

SESSION 8 (PP. 107–120):

What commitments did you make that you need to apply?

Be sure to finish the last five devotions!

DIG DEEPER THIS WEEK:
Read chapters 14–15 (pp. 196–222) in *The Resolution for Men*.

PRAYER

Spend some time praying for the guys in your group. Ask God to
help you not only hear the Word, but be doers of the Word. Enlist His
support in following through with the commitments you have made.

Day 1

ACKNOWLEDGE GOD'S GIFTS
FIRST CORINTHIANS 4:7

As you conclude this study, resolve to be a courageous man of God who wants to honor Him with your life. Remember, you have been greatly blessed. While you may not be the richest person in the world, you have been showered with blessings. Take time to reflect on God's provisions.

What are some of the financial blessings in your life? Relational blessings? Spiritual blessings?

While those gifts are very different, they share an origin. Read James 1:17 and 1 Corinthians 4:7.

Scripture teaches that we have nothing we did not receive. All our blessings come from God. Our spouses. Kids. Homes. Cars. Food. Your paycheck—a gift from God that could be taken away at any moment!

Paul warns us not to boast as if we had earned all these gifts on our own merits rather than received them as blessings. If we act like we deserve all the credit for our blessings instead of acknowledging them as gifts from the Lord's hand, we take the glory away from God. We rob Him of the recognition He deserves.

Every good thing you have came from God's hand. Thank Him today for all of His blessings. Make sure that you give Him the credit—including as you talk with your family and other people—for all of His good gifts to you.

Day 2

GIFTS AND A PLACE TO SERVE
ROMANS 12:3-8

Hopefully, through this study, you have become connected with men and families in a local church. In a few days, this study will come to an end. You don't need to try to live as a man of resolution on your own. Your church is a wonderful expression of God's grace and, while it is not perfect, it is God's vehicle for making disciples—ever-learning students of Christ who are growing more like Jesus.

> You need your church and your church needs you! Read Romans 12:3-8 to see your role. What great truth or application can you take from these verses?
>
> Verse 3:
> Verse 4:
> Verse 5:

Paul reminds us that we each have a gift and a place to serve in the body. In many churches, women comprise the majority of servants in volunteer positions. While we praise God for women's gifts and dedication, God calls men to be model servants and to step into leadership in their local congregations. You may be surprised to find what God can do through you as you step up to the plate!

Remember, God has gifted you specifically. You are a part of the body and have a God-planned purpose and role.

> What are you passionate about? How do you feel God has gifted you?

Day 3

LIVING AND ACTIVE

HEBREWS 4:12

As a man of resolution, you know the importance of committing to obey God's Word. Decisions become more clear-cut when you hold them up to the lens of Scripture. God's Word is more than adequate to provide direction and focus for every aspect of your life (see 2 Tim. 3:16-17).

> Read Hebrews 4:12. What do you think it means
> by describing God's Word as "living"? "Effective"?
> "Able to judge the ideas and thoughts" of our hearts?

God's Word is alive and well and can speak to you every time you open it. The Bible tells us about God—and how we should live in light of God as Lord of our lives. As you read its words, Scripture cuts through all of life's messes and distractions to convict you to evaluate your motives, which reside in the deepest places of your heart.

Do you believe every word in the Bible? Have you read every word in the Bible? Don't just rely on what others have said. As this study concludes, commit to studying the totality of Scripture.

> Turn to your Bible's contents page. List three Bible books
> with which you are most familiar.

> List three Bible books you have not yet explored.

Commit to renewing your love for the familiar and to exploring messages in less well-known Bible books. Know that God will open up new treasures for you. Ask Him to give you a lifelong hunger for His Word.

Day 4

GOD'S WILL FOR YOU
EPHESIANS 5:15-17

"The phrase 'the will of God' can sound very mysterious, like a code to be broken or a puzzle to be figured out, but it is actually another way to describe 'what God wants.' His will is described as both a way of living our lives that brings Him the most *pleasure* as well as His master *plan* for our lives that will bring Him the most glory" (*The Resolution for Men*, p. 206). Be assured that there is One who wants you to know His will even more than you want to know it—God Himself!

Find part of God's will for you in Ephesians 5:15-17.

These aspects of God's will are very simple: be wise in how you spend your days. Revolve your life around pleasing Him. The time we live in is evil, full of many things that can take us off course in honoring God and being a dedicated follower of Christ, a faithful husband, and a responsible father.

We understand God's will through the lens of His Word. Before concluding this devotion, flip back through the pages of this book. Basing your answers on what you have learned each week, record three things you know are God's will for your life.

God's will for me is to ...

God's will for me is to ...

God's will for me is to ...

Day 5

HOW TO LOSE YOUR LIFE
MATTHEW 10:32-39

Today's final devotion encourages you to stand firm on the resolves you have made during this study. Often at a time like this, you may say something like, "I'm ready to get my life back," or, "I'm trying to put my life back together." If that is your desire, you may have missed the point. Rather than getting your life back, seek to lose it instead.

Read the words of Jesus in Matthew 10:32-39.

At first glance, Jesus appears to challenge the Resolutions discussed in this study. Instead, He wants to reorient your focus. If you seek to please your wife or your children, you could forsake Jesus. But if you seek to please Jesus, you will always give your best to your wife and your children as a natural extension of your allegiance to Him. That's what it means to lose your life.

Surrender everything you have to Christ and let Him direct your paths, and you will gain the abundance of real life. Get introspective. Let God paint a picture of what your life could look like if you completely surrendered to Him.

If you loved Jesus more than anything else, how would your wife benefit? Your coworkers? Your children? Your church?

Commit your way to Jesus and follow Him wholeheartedly. See what He can do with a life that is fully surrendered to Him. To God be the glory!

THE
RESOLUTION
for MEN

I no longer live, but Christ lives in me.
The life I now live in the body,
I live by faith in the Son of God, who
loved me and gave Himself for me.

GALATIANS 2:20

You can stay true to this Resolution by staying
poor in spirit and surrendered to Him, by turn-
ing loose and letting Him do it. He'll make you a
man who lives seven days a week for the glory of
God— not because you can, but because He can.

Life has always been, still is today, and always will be
all about Him. It has never been about us. But we
should revel in the awesome privilege of aiming all
our passions and the rest of our days at living to bring
Him honor. The finale of all things is the glory of God.

THE RESOLUTION FOR MEN

The Locks and Keys of Effective Prayer

THE LOCKS: Ten Things That Block Prayer

1. **PRAYING WITHOUT KNOWING GOD THROUGH FAITH IN CHRIST.** Jesus said, "I am the way, and the truth, and the life; no one comes to the Father but through Me" (John 14:6). If a man hasn't been saved and surrendered to Christ as Lord, he has no mediator between himself and God and is unwelcome in the holy of holies (1 Tim. 2:5).

2. **PRAYING WITH AN UNREPENTANT HEART.** If you hold on to sin and refuse to confess it, you cannot take full hold on God (see Ps. 66:18-19).

3. **PRAYING FOR SHOW.** Prayers can be made in public, but only sincere hearts connect with God (Matt. 6:5).

4. **PRAYING REPETITIVE, EMPTY WORDS.** Why do we think God wants to hear canned, lifeless, unthinking prayers? (See Matt. 6:7-8.)

5. **PRAYERS NOT PRAYED.** It seems obvious, but one of the reasons our prayers don't get answered is because we never got around to praying them (see Jas. 4:2).

6. **PRAYING WITH A LUSTFUL HEART.** God isn't fooled by prayers that are more about how we can fulfill our sinful desires than how we can honor Him and fulfill His purposes (see Jas. 4:3).

7. **PRAYING WHILE MISTREATING YOUR SPOUSE.** Based on 1 Peter 3:7, if you don't listen to your wife, then God won't listen to you.

8. **PRAYING WHILE IGNORING THE POOR.** If we do not cultivate a generous, compassionate heart, we become spiritually impoverished and God ignores us (see Prov. 21:13).

9. **PRAYING WITH BITTERNESS TOWARD ANOTHER.** Unforgiveness indicates a closed, resistant heart in us, which closes off our prayer life (see Mark 11: 25-26).

10. **PRAYING WITH A FAITHLESS HEART.** If we don't really believe He cares or will answer, then He says He won't (see Jas. 1:6-8).

THE KEYS: Ten Things That Make Prayer Effective

1. **PRAYING BY ASKING, SEEKING, AND KNOCKING.** We should be specific and persistent and keep praying until something happens (see Matt. 7:7-8,11).

2. **PRAYING IN FAITH.** When followers of Christ believe He can and will, then He likely will . . . in His way and in His timing. He invites us to be bold enough to ask for big things (see Mark 11:24).

3. **PRAYING IN SECRET.** When we pray alone, God knows it is not for show. Seek to be close to Him even when no one is watching (see Matt. 6:6).

4. **PRAYING ACCORDING TO GOD'S WILL.** When we pray for what God wants more than for what we want, He will answer us. You can ask for whatever you want, but you should trust His response since He knows what you really want and need better than you do (see 1 John 5:14).

5. **PRAYING IN JESUS' NAME.** When we know Christ, we pray based upon His name, His reputation, His authority, and His track record, not our own worthiness (see John 14:13-14).

6. **PRAYING IN AGREEMENT WITH OTHER BELIEVERS.** United prayer works. To agree means to make a harmonious symphony. We pray in different ways, but we intercede together for the same result (see Matt. 18:19-20).

7. **PRAYING WHILE FASTING.** Come with a heart that is hungry and thirsty for God (see Acts 14:23).

8. **PRAYING FROM AN OBEDIENT LIFE.** An obedient heart is unashamed and at home in His presence, not afraid of being found out, not holding anything back (see 1 John 3:21-22).

9. **PRAYING WHILE ABIDING IN CHRIST AND HIS WORD.** God's Word renews our minds and aligns our prayers with His heart and mind (see John 15:7).

10. **PRAYING WHILE DELIGHTING IN THE LORD.** When we are satisfied with Him alone, He feels free to give us things we wanted to pursue but did not seek (see Ps. 37:4).

Adapted from *The Love Dare* (Nashville: B&H Publishing Group, 2008), 202–05.

How to Find Peace with God

God created us to please and honor Him. But because of our pride and selfishness, every one of us has fallen short and dishonored God at different times in our lives. We have all sinned against Him, failing to bring Him the honor and glory He deserves from each of us (Rom. 3:23). This includes your children too.

God is holy, so He must reject all that is sinful (Matt. 13:41-43). Because He is perfect, He cannot allow our sin against Him to go unpunished, or else He would not be a just judge (Rom. 2:5-8). The Bible says that our sins separate us from God and that the "wages of sin is death" (Rom. 6:23). This death is not only physical but also spiritual, resulting in separation from God for eternity.

Out of His love and kindness for us, God sent His only Son, Jesus Christ, to die in our place and shed His blood to pay the price for our sins. Jesus' death satisfied the justice of God while providing a perfect demonstration of His mercy and love (Rom. 5:8; John 3:16). Three days later, God raised Him to life as our living Redeemer to prove that He is the Son of God (Rom. 1:4; Eph. 2:1-7).

He commands all people everywhere to repent and turn away from their sinful ways and humbly trust Jesus for their salvation. By surrendering your life to His lordship and control, you can have forgiveness and freely receive everlasting life (Rom. 10:9).

Is anything stopping you from surrendering your life to Jesus right now? If you understand your need to be forgiven and are ready to begin a relationship with God, we encourage you to pray now and trust your life to Jesus Christ. Be honest with God about your mistakes and your need for His forgiveness. Resolve to ask Him to help you turn from your sin and to place your trust in Him and in what He did on the cross. Then invite Him into your life to fill you, change your heart, and take control.

If you are unsure how to communicate your desires to Him, then use this prayer as a guide:

> *Lord Jesus, I know I have sinned against You and deserve the judgment of God. I believe that You died on the cross to pay for my sins. I choose now to ask for Your forgiveness. Jesus, I'm making You the Lord and Boss of my life. Change me and help me now to live the rest of my life for You. Thank You for giving me a home in heaven with You when I die. Amen.*

Here are some important next steps to take as a new Christian.

1. Find a Bible-teaching church and ask to be baptized as an expression of your new commitment in Him. Start attending on a regular basis, sharing life with other believers in Jesus Christ.

2. Locate a Bible you can understand and begin to read it for a few minutes every day. Start in the Gospel of John and work through the New Testament. Ask God to teach you how to love Him and walk with Him. Begin to talk with God in prayer—thanking Him for your new life, confessing your sins when you fail, and asking for what you need.

3. Take advantage of the opportunities God gives you to share your faith with others. There is no greater joy than to know God and to make Him known!

4. If you have received God's forgiveness for your sins through faith and by His grace—whether now or many years ago—share this wonderful news with your family and children.

---

1. Adapted from Appendix V, "How to find peace with God," *The Love Dare for Parents* (Nashville, B&H Publishing. 2013).

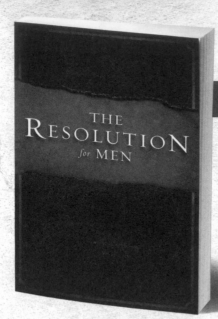

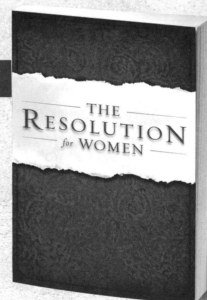